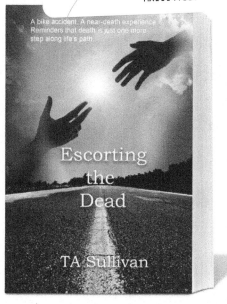

A bike accident. A near-death experience.
Reminders that death is just one more
step along life's path.

Escorting
the
Dead

TA Sullivan

Read how a bicycle accident and near-death experience changed my life along with my understanding of life and death. How out of that experience came the job of escorting the dead to the afterlife. A job that's filled with as much heartache as it is joy.

It's a job that has taught me a lot about compassion and love, but most of all it's taught me that death is merely another step along life's path.

Awards and Endorsements

*Twice Recipient of the Gold Non-Fiction Author's
Awards for Excellence!*

*Recipient of the Gold Non-Fiction Author's Book Award
for Excellence!*

*Recipient of the IMLP Non-Fiction Superior Award of
Writing Excellence.*

Other award-winning books from this author include:

All About Auras
All About Auras Reference Guide
On Dreams and Dream Symbols
Mastering Meditation
Choices
Life and Nature Volumes 1 & 2 (photos and poetry free e-book)

And fiction books:

The Starstone
The Globe of Souls
The Past Rekindled (a paranormal romance)
The Whimsy of Life (children's book free e-book)

All works are available at most online and paperback book merchants.

"Fantastic book! I'd love to read any books by this author after this one." Heritage Springs Daily News

"This is a very enjoyable book and a fast read." Lightner Book Reviews

"Intelligent and well-written book providing insight and hope." Mountain Journal Reviews

Mastering Meditation

"Loved the variety of meditation techniques included in this book." Star Journal

"Extremely informative and helpful, especially for beginners." Spiritual Awakening

"Although I've been meditating for a number of years, I still found some interesting new information in this book." Morningstar Mountain Journal

Choices

"This is so uplifting and so true." A Spiritual Life Book Reviews

"I loved the anecdotes and examples...very helpful in working through relationship issues." Family Health Magazine

"Extremely profound. The advice was so helpful." Heritage Springs Daily News

The Past Rekindled

"Steamy and dreamy. Can't wait for the next one…"
Hearts & Flowers Books4U

"The heroine is bright and breezy. Lovely!" Tri-Town
News

"Hot. Inventive. Intriguing." Rom-Book Reviews

The Starstone

"This is definitely a writer worth reading…I can't wait for
the second installment of this series." Daily News

"A fun way to spend a weekend. Unexpected characters
and enough plot twists to keep you guessing." Sunday
Journal

"Wow…fascinating and fun!" Courier News

The Globe of Souls

"Even better than the first book." Tri-Town News

"Funtastic fantasy with wit, charm, and action!" Fantasy
News Blog

"The author's take on fairies is unique…even more fun than her inventive take on elves in the first book." Book Journal

& * & * &

Keywords: near-death experience, NDE, reincarnation,
paranormal, spirituality, life and death, heaven, self-
improvement

& * & * &

Cover design by DL – Design and Digital Art
& * & * &

Author's note: Names and other identifying information, such
as occupations, professions, or geographical locations have been
changed. Otherwise, the events and interactions stated and
described in this book are reproduced as accurately as memories
allow them to be.

ISBN: 13: 9781072001447
BISAC: OCC034000

Acknowledgements

To my husband, the most loving person I know.
To my great friend Anna, she always understood.
To my sister-in-law, who encouraged me to finish this.
To Cathie my mentor and long-time friend.
And to everyone who has ever lost a friend or loved one.

Table of Contents

Is There Life After Death?

HAVE YOU EVER thought about what happens when we die? Most of us have, I'm sure. Every time someone in your social circle dies—friend, relative, co-worker, acquaintance—you wonder. Even when it's someone you merely read about in the news, there's still that fleeting wonder of whether there is something more, something beyond this life, waiting for them. Waiting for you.

Maybe it's about time that we brought death out of the coffin (so to speak). Maybe, if we pull back the shroud, we'll see that what lies beyond isn't as frightening as we think. Maybe, the image of a grim reaper coming forth from its stygian depths to spirit us away isn't as far off as we'd like to believe, yet death certainly isn't as bleak and intimidating as we fear, either.

And do we even really know what death is? According to the dictionary, death is the state of non-being. However, logic, common sense, science, and religion all tell us that there is no such state. They all say that although the physical form ceases to function, another part of us lives on; therefore, you can never not be.

That part of us that continues to exist is referred to by religion as the soul, the core, essence, the spirit, and the chi; while science calls it the psyche, the aura, a vibrational frequency, and a type of energy. Whatever name you give it, something of us remains once the body ceases to be. So, death is just an altered state of being, a state in which matter ceases to function, but awareness continues.

Therefore, while the person we knew and interacted with is no longer available to us, although we can no longer pick up a phone and call or text them, receive emails from them, or see their smiling face, they still exist. Just not in a state we recognize.

But where do they exist? In what form do they exist? Why can't we see them, hear them, or interact with them?

Afterlife Beliefs

Every culture, religion, family, or tribe has their own way of answering those questions—and sometimes they have even more than one answer.

The Mayans believed that the underworld had nine layers and their version of heaven had thirteen layers.

The Ancient Egyptians conceived of an afterlife that was quite similar to normal physical existence. The model for this new existence was the journey of the Sun. At night, the Sun descended into the Duat (the underworld). Eventually the Sun met the body of the mummified Osiris, and Osiris and the Sun, re-energized by each other, rose to a new life for another day. For the deceased, their body and their tomb were their personal Osiris and Duat.

Today, the beliefs are as myriad as the stars above. Most Christians believe in some form of heaven, complete with angels, cherubs, heavenly choirs, and a long-bearded, robed man waiting at the entrance to a large golden gate. They also believe in hell; a place that is depicted as being either torridly hot or frigidly cold and containing pitch-fork laden, goat-eyed, horned, and tailed half-men whose only job is to provoke them.

Meanwhile, many of those who follow Wicca, Hinduism, Judaism, and other similar religions believe that at death the dying consciousness of the body moves immediately to a new biological structure (usually another human body, although some believe that the consciousness can be reborn as an animal, plant, or insect) where it continues the cycle of lives with little interruption. For these people, an eternal afterlife only occurs once all the levels of physicality have been completed.

For others, there is no afterlife at all. Life simply ends when the body dies, and that's it. Still others believe that the afterlife is simply one step removed from our own world, sharing the same space as our world, but not viewable (except by a few chosen who see and speak to spirits). They believe that everyone who dies just watches over us while waiting for us to join them.

And just maybe that's why we're so frightened. There are so many possibilities, so many beliefs, that we don't know what to think. We start second-guessing ourselves and wondering what's real. Are our loved ones in heaven (or hell), or is that just a platitude that others tell us to comfort us during our bereavement? Do people really come back as someone or something else, or are they hanging around, just out of sight, waiting for us physicals to notice them (can you imagine just how crowded that would make their reality)?

But just because we aren't sure what type of world exists beyond our own, doesn't mean that some type of afterlife doesn't exist. Science has suggested that there are layers to our reality that we haven't fully grasped. And many doctors and their patients are convinced that they have witnessed the afterlife when declared clinically dead, and then returned to life through the miracles of modern medicine.

Cemeteries – Cities of the Dead

As a child when we drove past a cemetery, I would often comment, "Most of my friends are dead, you know."

I'm fairly certain that the first time I said that my parents must have freaked out. But what I remember most, is me making the remark and them rolling their eyes before glancing at each other with that Oh-well-it's-just-Tricia-being-Tricia looks.

Years later when I said something similar while driving with my then boyfriend (now spouse), he simply looked at me and replied, "So, did you want to stop and say 'Hello'?"

I swear that just made me love him more (and maybe that explains why we've been together nearly 40 years...he gets me).

The point though, is that even as a child I understood that death wasn't something scary or forever. Death was (and is) just another state of being—albeit one we can't easily relate to in our current state of physicality. However, if we remain quiet in our mind, emotions, and spirit, we can hear those who are no longer in physical form. We can hear them as they try to communicate with us using projected thoughts and memories, soft touches, vague ghostly images, or even physical and non-physical symbols (such as pennies, long-lost items suddenly appearing again, or mental images retained from dreams or meditations).

They want us to understand that death isn't a void or a vast darkness of nothingness. Dying is a transitioning to another state of being; a state of being at Home. Home...a place of loving acceptance and continued mental and spiritual growth and enlightenment.

In fact, I've received messages from several loved ones that have gone home to the astral plane from a non-professional medium friend. I've included the non-personal part of these messages here.

Two of the messages are from people who offered me support and encouragement when I needed it most, while the third message is from my writing mentor and high-school friend.

AJ: "Tell Trish that I love her and I'm glad that she has decided to share this information with others. "She's always been intuitive and sensitive…sometimes too sensitive. I mean, sometimes she had difficulty separating herself from the emotions of those around her."

Q: What's it like over there, AJ? Is it what you thought it would be?

"What's it like over here? It's hard to put into words. It's heaven, but not the literal heaven that comes with angels, clouds, and harps.

"It's structured, but not formal. Everyone comes and goes participating in lessons, tasks, jobs, or entertainments of their choice.

"I've been studying with several of the masters learning how to bend light and mix it with emotions to create different harmonics.

"I've also been studying different time/spaces on the physical plane to determine which one I might like to return to. Each one has potential, but I need to decide which one will best help me with my goals."

JB: "It's been hard. Mostly because I haven't completely let go. I keep coming down [to the lower levels of the astral plane] to watch my family. I worry about them.

"I've been collaborating with my guide (Jason). He's been helping me work through some of my left-over issues.

"We've also been deciding on my next incarnation. There are several other fragments that I'm working with on this. We want to find a reality where we can try the doctor/patient lesson. It's been a while since I've played doctor. [laughter and happy energy]

"We're thinking East coast late 1800's or early 1900's. We'll see what the others have to say."

Cathie Baumgardner (Cathie Linz): "I really don't recommend dying from cancer too often. It really is painful. But it allowed me to complete the monad with the soul acting as my mother there in your world.

"She needed to care for me, and she did all my life. Even when her own health was at stake, she cared for me.

"I've been working through some issues with my guide and other fragments from previous incarnations. Lately, we've been discussing books. That's one of the reasons I came when you asked.

"I still love books, and I appreciate what you have to say. I've spent numerous lives with books. I've lived as a scribe, as a librarian, as an author, and as voracious readers. But few of the books I've interacted with have had the audacity of this book.

"Keep writing, and most of all, keep writing truth."

Show Me the Proof

DEATH.

That word probably frightens people more than any other.

Why?

Because it represents the "great unknown." We know less about death than we do about outer space or the deep recesses of Earth's oceans. After all, it's not easy to explore a dimension or state of being that requires us to cease living. So, for most of us, death becomes the area that, like on maps of old, was marked with the words: "There be monsters here."

MONSTERS. DEMONS. ANGELS.

These are what we think of when we think about death, because that's all we know, or at least suspect, based on the stories that we are told about the land of beyond. Of course, some people eschew the typical concept of death being a place or a continuation of some form of life. Instead, they see death as a black nothingness. These are the ones that are convinced that you live once and that's it.

However, there are others who divide the realm of death into two states: one where demons and monsters abide, and another where angels and cherubs live.

But the one thing missing from all their beliefs is…

PROOF

Of course, trying to prove whether there is a type of life after the physical body dies isn't easy to do. After all, how do you gather statistics and measurements when you have no physical form?

It is just this conundrum that has plagued most of us who have died and returned. We have garnered little acceptance from the scientific community regarding our experiences simply because we lack the physical proof of what occurred. All we have is our memory of the events, and even those vary widely based on each person's perceptions and interpretations. For instance, those who are strict Catholics often see their experiences through the filter of their Catholic iconography and tenets; while those who are atheists may describe their experiences using a filter of science or space aliens.

Some experiments have been conducted. They are usually of the sort wherein someone is forced into a chemically- or electronically induced death, and then revived within the time limits deemed safe. While these experiments are done in the confines of labs and under the supervision of "specialists," the interpretation of what did or did not occur on the other side (if indeed, the other side was even reached) is still up to the individual who died.

The specialists monitoring the physical side of the experiment can note data on the traveler's body—heart rate, brain waves, blood pressure, etc.—however, they are unable to experience what the traveler who died experienced.

Scientists can cite all types of speculation and theories to explain what may or may not have occurred—low oxygen levels in the brain, random electrical pulses, or hallucinations induced by some latent chemical reaction in the dying body—but without proof of whether the dead person actually traveled anywhere, their suppositions are as bogus as their disdain of what the travelers experienced.

So, even though I've been to the other side a multitude of times (because not only have I experienced a near-death episode, but I also function as a psychopomp for others—both of which I explain in this book), I understand the skepticism. I know that until we devise some sort of carrier to ferry us (the physical us) into the realm of death and back, all any of us has is our own beliefs as to what awaits us when we die.

To that end, I have written my interpretation of my near-death experience, as well as my experiences as a psychopomp (or death escort). I do this with the hope that this book can help people overcome some of their fear of death. Because death isn't anything to fear.

Death is merely another step along life's path.

What is a Psychopomp?

JUST WHAT IS a psychopomp, anyway? When I looked it up in the dictionary it said that the term psychopomp came from the Greek word *psuchopompos*, and literally means, *the guide of souls*.

That is such a lovely expression, don't you think? A *guide of souls*; someone to guide the deceased to their new existence; someone to help them make the transition from physical being to spiritual being. What a comforting thought, to know that there is someone there to help us make that transition.

As I continued looking for information on psychopomps, I found that most records identify a psychopomp as either someone who has already crossed over or is alive but acting in spirit form.

Either way, psychopomps operate on a spiritual plane, which may account for why they are regarded as something mysterious and myth-like, rather than as something real and easily substantiated. After all, how many of us are truly accepting of things we can't see, taste, hear, touch, and measure? Most of us like a good monster story, but few of us actually believe in monsters. Why? Because we haven't seen, heard, or touched one.

However, the idea of escorts or guides for the dead has been around since humans started recording history. The concept appears in songs, stories, art, and books of both a secular and religious nature. It is an especially common concept in religions of all types.

Symbols and images of the dead being carried or led away by others (in human and non-human form) are often used in funerary art. Sometimes the dead must board a boat, chariot, or other vehicle, and other times the escort (especially those depicted in animal form) merely carries the dead person away.

The concept of escorts for the deceased can be found in Africa, from Ancient Egypt to modern Zimbabwe; in the Americas, from the Aztecs and Inuit to the modern-day businessman. The concept is also seen in Asia and Malaysia, as well as Europe and Polynesia.

The concept of death escorts also appears in every religion from Bha'i to Zoroastrianism. While in some instances, psychopomps have been depicted as human spirits, such as the image of Hermes that appears on some of the Greek funerary vessels found in museums; in other instances, death escorts have been assigned the forms of ravens, crows, sparrows, hyenas, jackals, wolves, banshees, or large, black dogs (such as in the Harry Potter series).

Perhaps these depictions had a lot to do with the beliefs of the time. Back in the day, many people didn't understand the nature of carrion birds, hyenas, or wolves. When carrion eaters (such as ravens, crows, jackals, or hyenas) would appear near the areas of battles and illness, it was easy to personify and associate them with the transitioning of the souls from death to the afterlife.

Each culture from ancient times until the present develops their own version of a psychopomp—the Greeks had Hermes, and the Japanese, Shinigami. We all need a way to explain those things we don't understand. We need a way to fit things into our mental picture of the world.

Today, most of us include angels in our world view. Therefore, the most common description of a modern psychopomp is as a type of angel. They are usually described as having a glowing body, or sometimes a gold or silvery aura that encapsulates all or part of the body. Only about half of the sources that I researched also include wings in the description, and those sources that do are not confined to any specific religious group.

Some religious and secular groups that include angels in their vocabulary describe them as: *a supernatural being or spirit acting as a guiding influence or a guardian*; while the dictionary defines an angel as: *a benevolent celestial being that acts as an intermediary between heaven and earth, especially in Christianity, Judaism, Islam, and Zoroastrianism.*

It doesn't take much to extend that description to cover the escorting of spirits from life to death (or from death to life if you believe in reincarnation).

It seems to me that as man has changed, so has his description of death escorts. However, the belief in such a being hasn't changed or diminished; instead, it continues to persist.

So why aren't death escorts part of the story we're told to make us feel better about someone's death? How do we know psychopomps aren't just figments of Aunt Mary's illness when she claims to see angels standing in the corners of her hospital room?

I can't really answer the first question. But regarding the second one…I know death escorts are real, because I am one.

Why be a Death Escort?

SO, WHY DOES someone become a death escort?
There are probably as many reasons as there are death
escorts. That's because the reasons are different for
each of us. For some it's a calling, much like some
people who accept a spiritual or religious mantle here
in the physical world. For others it's all about the
challenge, and for still others, it's a learning
experience. For me it's partially because of the
learning experience, and partially my desire to feel
useful and needed.

As to how you become a death escort–that's
easy…you choose it. This isn't something that is
foisted on you; it's not something that you *have* to do.
Each soul who takes this on does so because they want
to.

For most people, the decision to take on this task is
done during one of their astral periods between lives.
This is also why during their physical life, there is no
memory or knowledge of this information. We all take
the "forget everything pill" before jumping back to
Earth and another lifetime. So, little (if anything) is
remembered of what occurred before the current life.

For me, I agreed to take on this task about seven lifetimes ago. So, I've been learning and growing and developing my skills for quite some time.

I Want to Teach

FROM THE TIME I was little, all I ever wanted to do was teach. In fact, as a child one of my favorite pastimes was playing school. Most of the time, my only pupils were my dolls, but that didn't matter.

Of course, at that age, I thought that the only way to teach was by being a schoolteacher. Therefore, my favorite books were the *Little House on the Prairie* series. I wanted to be Laura Ingalls and teach school in a little one-room schoolhouse.

As I got older, and my reluctance to follow the rules became more evident, I thought perhaps becoming a nanny would be more appropriate. Less red-tape and interference as to what and how the lessons were taught. (Yes, I'll admit it, I was hardly in touch with reality; but then, what 12- or 13-year-old is?)

It wasn't until I took off for college that I realized that what I wanted to teach had little to do with reading, writing, and 'rithmatic. What I needed to share was something much more intrinsic to the basics of life. This meant the standard forms of teaching wouldn't accommodate the types of lessons and information that I wanted to convey. Therefore, I would have to find some other way to distribute my message.

Aha Moments

Almost everyone has experienced at least one "aha moment." It's that moment when you finally understand some concept or idea you've been struggling with.

I've had two such "aha moments."

When I was a tweener, my mother gave me a book. She told me I would find it interesting. It didn't look like anything special—just a simple paperback book with a blue cover.

When I opened it and began to read, I was hooked. It was filled with new concepts and ideas that somehow also felt familiar. It was an interesting read, and I knew I would want to read it again. I felt the truth of the information, although I didn't fully comprehend everything.

I set the book aside, and life went on. Meanwhile, the concepts and ideas percolated at the back of my mind, popping out now and again when something I was doing, or something being said, made me think, "I've heard or read that before."

I never consciously thought about the book until years later when I hit an emotional crossroads. At that point, I thought that something in that book just might help me with my choices.

I searched high and low for the book, sure that I had placed it in one of the many bookcases in the house, but I couldn't find it anywhere. Unable to locate it, I asked my mother about it. She had no idea what I was talking about. She said she had never seen nor read such a book.

That night, confused and still positive that the book existed, I went to bed. I stood in the library, the blue book in my hand, only this time I knew it was a dream. I read the book through, several times, and when I put it aside, I had my first "aha moment."

It was as if I had been stumbling around in a darkened house, before suddenly finding the main fuse box. I felt lit up. I not only understood everything the book had said, but I recognized the truth of the concepts and ideas I had read.

This aha moment also gave me the awareness I needed to better understand what the kaleidoscope of colors that surrounded people meant. Now, not only could I see that everyone had a beautiful rainbow surrounding them, I discovered that I could "read" most of the information contained in the different layers.

The Second Aha Moment

I was sitting on the grass, the sun warming my back while the trees murmured to each other. A gentle breeze caressed my cheek, and the droning of bees filled the air. Although, I noted all of this on one level,

I didn't really notice it at all. The book in my lap occupied my complete attention, holding me, captivating me. Fascinated, I clung to every word.

As I read through it, I felt a rightness about the world and universe. It was as if each word only confirmed what I already knew. There was so much truth and wisdom packed into this thin, white volume, that I was amazed. How could this little book contain so much truth and wisdom?

I couldn't stop reading. Each word was a delight. Each sentence was a treat that filled my senses and teased my mind. Each page filled my mind with a million thoughts and ideas. They flooded through me, rolled over me, and barreled on past as I tried desperately to hang on to them. Every unique idea burst through me like a barrage of skyrockets, and I felt as if I were soaring high above the world.

My eyes moved down the page, and my mind continued to buzz and thrum with all the delightful insights that each sentence called forth from my being. Where had this book been hiding? Why hadn't I found it until now? Everyone needed to read this book, I thought as I pulled my eyes from the page and smiled up at the butterflies soaring above me.

I thought of all the people who could be helped just by reading any portion of this magnificent writing; of all the wars and other violent situations that could be averted if people would just read from this book. It was dumbfounding that more people hadn't learned what I had just from the few moments I had spent reading this book.

With my finger holding my place in the book, I stood and looked toward the house. I needed to make copies of this book, so everyone would have a chance to see what I had seen. As I glided through the grass toward the house, I suddenly awoke.

I sat up in the bed and searched frantically for the book; but of course, it wasn't there. It had just been a dream. There was no actual book, there was only the information that each of us carries within ourselves. Not that this makes the information any less valid, but it does make it harder to share. After all, a physical book can be copied, or given away, or read to others. But how does one share the information that is written only on their own soul?

Somehow, I had to find a way to help people discover their own "book of knowledge." Even those who might be too afraid to read the book still needed to know that the book existed. So recognizing what I needed to teach became my second "aha moment."

Following My Intuition

ALL THROUGH MY growing years I had relied on my intuitive side to lead me, and high school and college were no different. In high school, I indulged my love of reading and writing by taking non-required classes in literature, creative writing, and journalism. I took the extra classes mostly because I enjoyed reading and writing, so I thought these classes would be fun. But I also took them because my intuition nagged at me that I would need these skills throughout my life. So, why not? It's always great when you can do something you love to do, and you know it's good for you, too.

Arriving at college, I again let my intuition lead the way. However, it led me away from the education and child development courses, which I would need if I wanted to fulfill my dream of teaching. I didn't understand why my intuition would do that. Teaching had been my dream from the very beginning; so, why would my intuition push me away from that?

Sometimes, if the information is important to my life—really important—not following my intuition can be like fighting my way through a vat of taffy. The negative energies created by going against a need that strong, can make me physically ill, too. It's my spiritual center's way of saying, "You NEED to listen to me."

Evidently, following a different path, a path other than the one I had planned on, was that important. Because every time I even tried to take myself into the teaching center to register for education courses, I became nauseated. I felt like I was walking against a hundred-mile-an-hour wind. Finally, I gave up trying to follow my plans, and I waited to see what intuition had planned.

I stood in the middle of the campus with my eyes closed, and eventually, I felt a tug. I followed that pull and ended up in front of the buildings where journalism and creative writing were taught. I had no idea how I could teach by becoming some sort of writer, but if this is what was wanted, then this was the path I would follow.

At one point in my sophomore year, I took some psychology courses and became enthralled. I thought becoming a psychologist or parapsychologist would be a great career; so, I signed up for more psychology courses. However, intuition didn't agree, and I was led—gently, but very determinedly—back to my writing path.

It was also about that time that I became involved with the campus newspaper and creative works journal. I was asked to research and write an article, which, when printed, had quite an impact. It was the first time something I had written made a visible difference in the world around me.

Up until then, I had written primarily poems and short stories. People who had read them told me they were nice, okay, or interesting; but I always felt they were just being polite. No one was moved by my words. No one cried or changed their life because of my words.

The publishing of this story was definitely different, though. The story actually did make some ripples. So, it became one of those "now I get it" moments that you often hear about.

As I walked to my classes, I would hear people talking about the article, and that's when I realized how impactful writing can be. It's also when I realized that writing can be a powerful teaching tool. Imagine writing some bit of wisdom or life insight and having hundreds, maybe even thousands of people read it? It was mind boggling.

Now I understood why I needed to become a writer and not just a classroom teacher. I needed to reach a bigger audience than was possible in a classroom, and I needed to impart a different type of lesson than the usual schoolroom curriculum allowed for.

Am I Teacher Yet?

ONCE OUT OF school, I needed to join the real world. But doing what? I knew that writing could help me change things, I'd seen that for myself. However, there seemed to be a bigger purpose here than just writing stories about bake sales and wedding announcements for the local paper.

Again, I followed my intuition. This usually amounted to focusing on a map of the area and asking about employment. When my intuition pinpointed a location, I would get in my car and let my intuition lead me to the building. The companies in that building would then receive copies of my resume, and within a week or two I would have a job.

Few of these jobs had anything to do with writing. However, what they did have in common was someone who was seeking spiritual inspiration or insights. After several of these encounters, I began to see a theme:

Writing + Teaching + Spirituality = Life Goal

For several years, I continued this path of single-person service. The exchange of ideas was heady. I was learning as much as I was teaching, and I loved it. Most of all, I was learning how to share this wealth of information with others I'd never met in person.

Each week I would take the flow of ideas that had been started due to one or more conversations, and I would write articles from various viewpoints as I tried to capture all the nuances of the different concepts.

These articles eventually made their way onto a website that I created. Now, I was getting email and questions from all around the world. Ideas I never would have considered were brought to my attention because of this web presence. I spent hours researching and reading because someone had an idea or a question.

This is what teaching was about, I thought. Sharing ideas, learning new concepts, and finding ways to look at the world through different eyes.

Awakening to Awareness

The more I learned, the more I knew. It's a logical progression. However, in this case, it was more of a "the more I learned, the more I remembered."

During this period in my life, I felt there was a hidden door inside of me that I was just now discovering. And each time a new concept, a new idea, or a new way of perceiving things was brought to me, it allowed me to build the key I needed to unlock that door.

I became like Harry Potter in *The Order of the Phoenix* when he continuously dreams of the door to the Department of Mysteries. Only in my case, I was dreaming of the door to all things before (this life).

When I was a child, my dreams were filled with the banal—I would dream of conversing with my teacher or one or more of my fellow students, and the next day that exact conversation would occur. The conversation wasn't anything Earth-shattering, nor was it even all that interesting. It was more along the lines of a student asking a question regarding the Civil War and the teacher answering the question—as I said, not all that interesting. Yet, my nights were filled with these types of "revelations."

It became so commonplace for me to dream of the next day's events, that sometimes I wondered why I should even bother going to school since I had already lived it. After all, if you've heard the conversation once, why hear it again?

When I went on to Middle School, one of the classes I had to take was typing. The first day of typing was horrible. I couldn't figure it out. The finger placement seemed totally alien, and the whole rhythm of the typing itself was like some foreign music that I simply didn't understand.

That night I dreamt of nothing but my fingers flying across the keyboard and the words magically appearing on the paper. The rhythm was no longer foreign; rather it seemed a part of my soul.

The next day when I stepped into typing class, my heart was racing, and I was sure everyone would be laughing at me again, as my fingers stumbled over the keystrokes. Instead, when the teacher told us to start the typing exercise, I was the first one done, and with absolutely no mistakes.

I couldn't believe it. Then, I remembered the nightlong dream filled with typing. That's when I realized that my prophetic dream was really an astral visit, and I had taught myself how to type—literally overnight. That's also when I began to see some use to these dreams. However, the use I foresaw, was not to be; primarily, because the dreams changed.

My dreams no longer showed me the day-to-day happenings of my life. Instead, my dreams became prophecies of events involving friends and family. However, not only did the theme of the dreams change, but so did the time frame for these occurrences. The dreams were no longer showing me what would happen the next day. Now, the events that I saw wouldn't occur until weeks or months into the future.

For instance, one night in my early 'tweens, I dreamt of my uncle. I saw him walk out his front door. He then went down the walkway toward his car, which was in the driveway. It was early morning in the dream, and he turned and gave a little wave to his wife. Then, as he turned back toward the car, he blew up. There was a flash of flame, the sound of an explosion, and then nothing. I sat straight up in bed, panting, and overwrought.

It took me several hours to calm down and go back to sleep. I didn't tell anyone because I wasn't sufficiently convinced that it was anything other than a nightmare. However, like most dreams, I did record it in my journal. Writing my dreams in a journal as soon as I awaken from them not only helps me remember them, but it also helps me calm down after a nightmare. So, although upset at first, by the time I had recorded it, I had convinced myself that it was nothing.

As life went on, the memory of that dream faded. However, two months later, I came home from school to a saddened household. My mother told me that my uncle had died that morning of a massive coronary.

I was horrified. I hadn't said anything to anyone about my dream because it seemed so silly. Now, I kept wondering if I should have said something. Perhaps I could have prevented his death. Maybe if I had said something, he could have seen a doctor, gotten a magic pill, or one of those operations that people had when their hearts were bad. Instead, I had done nothing.

For the longest time, I refused to allow myself to dream. I didn't want to know what was going to happen—good or bad. I mean, what good was it, when I couldn't stop good people from dying? As for the good news, well, most of the time it wasn't all that good, it was simply mundania from everyday life.

After about three years, though, I realized how cut off I felt. I felt like a part of me had been imprisoned. There was vital information out there that I wasn't getting because I wouldn't allow myself to, and I realized that I didn't like the feeling.

I needed and wanted that information—no matter how mundane it may seem. Somehow, those dreams kept me in contact with the entire world, with the universe at large. Without those dreams, I was deaf, dumb, and blind in a world full of sharp edges and unexpected pitfalls.

By allowing the dreams back into my waking life, I allowed myself to link up with and interact with many more people than I would have ever had the chance to meet here in the physical world. By allowing my waking self to remember my dreams again, I allowed myself to remember all the astral visits I was making.

I also allowed myself to begin remembering those prophetic dreams again. Even though I couldn't stop things from happening, most of the time, I still had ample warning so that I was able to make less emotional choices in response to the events. By having time to put some thought and contemplation behind my choices, I could more easily stay on the best path for me.

When I'm entering a new lesson, my dreams give me a little nudge or warning and when someone else has made an unexpected choice that is going to affect me, I also get warning dreams.

I've also listened for those dreams that told me when someone I knew was going to die. Because the dream of my uncle helped me understand that death is just another aspect of life, and everyone needs to experience both sides of that coin—life and death. Knowing about someone's choices ahead of time helps me be a bit more prepared, that's all.

Once I understood that death was a fact of life, another piece of the key clicked into place. But the final piece of the key appeared during a full solar eclipse.

Completing the Key

IT WAS A time of turmoil and strife in my family life, and I was emotionally drained. Nature has always been a refuge for me, and movement (especially repetitive movement) has always helped me relax. Therefore, I was spending a lot of time walking. Walking helped me cope with all my agitation and anxiety.

The day of the eclipse was just another day to me. Stressed and overwrought after getting more unwelcome news on the family front, and then having been yelled at by my boss regarding some client, I left work just before lunch break.

I drove to my favorite park for a walk. Mine was the only car in the lot, and I was glad. I was really in no mood to share the park with anyone else right then.

I rambled up hills and down, noticing little. My mind skittered from one topic to another, never staying long enough on any one to latch onto a cohesive idea. As my thoughts tumbled over each other, the shadows grew deeper around me. The day, which had been so bright just moments before, was suddenly cast into dusk. I looked up amazed to realize that the sun was nearly gone.

I had heard that there was supposed to be a full eclipse of the sun that day, but with my mind on so many other things, it didn't really seep into my consciousness until I was confronted with dusk at midday.

It only took a few more moments for the sun to be totally hidden behind the moon. Only the slimmest of the sun's edges remained, and even that was dimming rapidly. Soon it was dark—as dark as late evening, yet it was only a little past noon. I reached skyward as if to pluck the dark cover from the sun, and I felt, for a moment, as if my feet had literally left the ground.

Startled, I dropped my hand and looked back at myself. I stood on the darkened path with nothing but shadows gathered around me. I stared at my feet as if to reassure myself that they were still firmly planted on the pine straw-covered path.

Looking skyward again, I once more felt a compulsion to release my hold on the Earth and fly. I ran forward three steps and jumped, sure that I would find myself soaring through the heavens like some caped superhero. And in some ways, I did. Although, my feet never actually left the ground, to me it felt as if they had.

I was, somehow soaring miles above the Earth, racing with the clouds and looking down at the Earth from the heavens above. It was surreal, yet it felt as real to me as the body I wore. I hovered in a treetop and watched the world go by, then soared up into the clouds once again, to frolic with a flock of passing birds.

Just as the corona began to peek out from behind the cloaking moon, I saw a brilliant light before me. I reached out to touch it and it evaded my reach. I extended my arm as far as I could, and, just when I thought I would never be able to reach far enough, I touched it.

My whole being burst with a joyousness beyond words. At the same moment, the sun escaped its dark mask and the world was lit with a brilliance from both inside and out.

The next thing I remember was picking myself up off the ground where I lay at the base of a large old oak tree. I felt giddy and light-headed. I could barely maintain my balance, and my face was split by the biggest smile I could possibly wear.

I wanted to sing, to fly, to dance, to run, to twirl. I was blissful and ecstatic, and the feeling lasted for the rest of the day.

When people asked why I was smiling, I had no way to explain it. But it was infectious. Although I couldn't explain why I was smiling, everyone I encountered ended up smiling, too. It was impossible for me or anyone near me not to smile.

All bad feelings went on hiatus that day. I had touched my soul and soared with essence, and I was sharing those good feelings with everyone I came near.

I wanted that feeling to stay forever. It was the most wonderful feeling in the world. And somehow, I knew that if I wanted that feeling to happen again, I needed to unlock that door deep inside me. I needed to release those memories, because they would enable me to find the path back to that feeling.

Having touched my own soul, I was ready to see what was beyond this world. I was ready to fly untethered by the physical world that restrains us. I was ready to experience the next lesson.

What's Next?

EVEN WITH THE key, the door opened slowly. At first, there were small, incremental increases to my intuitiveness. I went from my normal gut instinct type of knowing (which told me little more than something was good, bad, or important), to knowing why (why is it important, how will it help or impact me). Soon, even that increased. I began to know (in a loose way) what someone in proximity to me was thinking or feeling.

That's when the next lesson occurred.

Being able to "hear" or sense other people's thoughts and emotions required me to learn the difference between my thoughts and emotions and those of the people around me. And it was probably one of the hardest skills I had to develop.

There were several times I walked away from a job or a friend because I was picking up on someone else's anger and discontent. But because I couldn't distinguish their feelings from mine, I assumed I was angry with the job or upset with the friend.

I remember one such instance very clearly. With

satchel, purse, and keys in hand, I walked into the office and over to my cube. I was putting my things in the lower left drawers of my desk when the phone rang. My day at work had begun.

I was busy typing one of the many contracts that our department was responsible for when my co-worker came in. She was agitated and upset, and soon, so was I. The boss came out and reprimanded her about something, which only made things worse. All morning long, the phrase, "I'm gonna quit" went through my brain like a mantra. By lunch, I was so angry (though I had no idea with whom or about what), that I walked up to my boss and told him I quit.

I grabbed my stuff from the bottom drawer and walked out the door. When I got home, my husband couldn't believe I had walked off my job. As we talked it through, I finally realized that it wasn't my idea to quit. The emotional energy had been coming from my co-worker. It had simply overwhelmed me until I was the one who had acted on it.

That incident led me to see the pattern that until then, I had kept missing. One minute I'd be having a relatively normal day, and the next I'd be agitated or ebullient in an out of proportion way to what was occurring around me.

If I left the area, I would soon return to my previously steady emotional state. Now, I could more easily identify when the emotions weren't mine. But I still had to learn how to cope with those emotions. I couldn't keep walking away from my office because someone else was having a difficult day. And if I didn't leave, I usually ended up saying or doing something that I then had to apologize for later.

But how to explain it to the boss, the friend, or any other people involved? How do I explain why I had done or said what I had? It wasn't like I could say, "It wasn't me. It just looked and sounded like me."

(Like that isn't nuts or anything.)

Split Vision

Other increases in my skills included knowing what the possible futures were of people, knowing what people I had never met or seen were feeling or doing, or sensing the atmosphere of a building—even when no one else was presently inside the building.

For most of these abilities, I was tuned into the astral plane, while still functioning here in the "real" world. This made my life a bit disconcerting.

Why disconcerting? Because many times I felt like I was walking in two different worlds, two different dimensions. I was no longer bound to just the physical world. I was straddling the line between here and there, and it was an odd experience. I was seeing two worlds, one overlaying the other, but neither of them was clear.

Imagine needing glasses and everything you look at is

just slightly out of focus. That's how I was seeing the world, all blurry and fuzzy. It took me a few stumbles and tumbles as I tripped over things that weren't really there or walked into doors that I hadn't noticed in the real world – that is, before I got used to separating the layers and seeing each world discretely.

I saw (and still do see) the world as a set of overlays. There was the physical world that I interacted with just like everyone else; but, layered on top of that was the shadow world of the astral plane. So, even when I was here in the physical, I was still tuned in to the astral.

It took a bit of practice to get to learn to cope with the dual vision. I had to consciously split my focus so that it was more 70-30, not 50-50 (70% to the reality I was in, 30% to the other one). However, the more I grew accustomed to this way of viewing things, the less I had to think about it. While I was learning, I ended up with a lot of bruises, but soon it just became natural to see the world this way.

Once I mastered it, I was absolutely thrilled. In fact, I was a little too proud of myself now that I had these abilities. I was so proud of myself that I spent hours showing off by doing readings for people whether they wanted them or not.

For instance, a woman in the office where I worked kept complaining about her boyfriends. She consistently selected a guy that was the epitome of manners and graciousness when they first dated. However, once the two of them became a steady item, the guy became a bully. He would belittle her (usually in front of family and friends), call her on the phone and yell at her, and he constantly told her how stupid she was.

One day, I decided to help. So, I did a reading for her. (Not that she asked for one; nor did she even know that I was doing it. I had just decided that I was going to help her see how to fix her life.)

It's amazing how irritated and hostile people can get when you give them information that they don't want, don't believe, and aren't ready to handle. At first, I was surprised and hurt at how ungracious she was.

Then when she refused to speak to me anymore, I was hurt and puzzled. Sometimes I can be surprisingly dense. However, the lesson eventually sank in: You are not the cosmic Dear Abby. So, I stopped showing off, and waited for intuition to tell me what was next.

The Door Opens

WHAT CAME NEXT was using the key to open the door. As it opened, my skill set grew. But the door didn't open easily. This was probably a good thing, as it gave me time to adjust to all the new skills and talents flourishing in me.

However, I eventually reached a point when the door wouldn't open any further. It had stuck about half-way and no matter how much I pushed, it remained stuck.

I was frustrated and relieved. Frustrated, because I wanted to know what else was behind there; relieved, because I was afraid to find out. If I pushed the door open any further, there was no going back. So, because my curiosity was as strong as my fear, the door remained stuck.

Sometimes, it takes an intense event to force a decision. That's what happened with that door. I was unable to overcome my indecision, and I needed an intense event to force myself to decide—open the door all the way or live with the fear and uncertainty of not knowing.

Sometimes the problems with being in tune with yourself and your universe is knowing too much about what's coming.

Hearing the Approach

FOR MOST PEOPLE, car accidents are just that—accidents. For me, they've always been events that I've known were going to happen. So, why not avoid them? Trust me, I've tried. I've tried often enough to realize that I couldn't run from something that I had obviously helped orchestrate.

For some inexplicable reason, a part of me had decided that vehicular collisions were a wonderful way to push myself into either making a decision or learning a lesson. (Yeah, I don't know what I was thinking when I made that choice, either.)

While I've reconciled myself to this, I'm still not sure why for months prior to the actual accident I must "hear" it approaching.

Just like always, this incident started with nightmares. I was in the car behind a line of traffic. Brake lights flashed in front of me, but I knew I couldn't stop in time. My heart pounded, and my mouth went dry. My head was thrown forward, and then back as the cars collided. Pain burned in my chest as it smashed into the steering wheel. Then I would awaken.

These dreams happened three or four nights a week for about a month. Then the dreams stopped. That's when the "auditory hallucinations" started. I began "hearing" car crashes— the squeal of brakes locking while tires skidded across pavement, followed by the rending and tearing of metal and the shattering of glass. Then came the musical tinkling of glass and metal as the pieces bounced onto the tarmac. I heard these sounds while reading, brushing my teeth, even when I was watching TV.

Initially, the sounds were so soft and so subtle that I barely noticed. However, they grew louder with each occurrence. By the end of the second month the noises had grown to the point that the sound was all around me. Soon, the sounds of the car accident blotted out everything else.

At the end of the third month, ghostly images started to appear with the sounds. I'd look in the mirror to put on my makeup and I'd see a hazy car accident happening behind me.

By the start of the fourth month, everything stopped. Completely and totally stopped. It was such a relief to have the images and noises gone that I was lulled into feeling safe.

The day of the accident was a glorious day—brisk but sunny, with that smell of turning leaves that can sometimes flavor late autumn. In fact, it was so beautiful that I just couldn't stay inside. All the warnings I had received flew out of my mind as I grabbed my bicycle. After all, I was going for a bike ride, not a drive.

I pedaled my way around the neighborhood keeping the golf course to my right. This was my way of making sure I could find my way home since we had just moved to the neighborhood, and I wasn't that familiar with the streets.

My hair fluttered behind me. I had no helmet on; I had grown up in an era where scrapes and bruises were worn like badges of honor. Helmets and safety pads hadn't existed when I was growing up, and being way past the age of childhood, I hardly felt the need to start wearing them now.

I coasted down a small hill toward a cross street. I saw a van approaching the 2-way stop sign for the cross street but gave it little thought. This was a quiet community with lots of kids, so I fully expected the van's driver would stop at the stop sign. However, the van's driver didn't meet my expectations. I was halfway across the intersection when the van collided with me.

I can almost laugh now looking back on the experience and remembering the look of shock on the face of the van's driver. When he hit me and my bike, the impact lifted me off the bike seat and onto the hood of the van. I'm sure my look of panic and astonishment was at least equal to that of his. His eyes and mine met, and locked. What I remember is his wide brown eyes staring at me with a larger O below formed by his dropping jaw.

The bike was mangled by the van as it continued forward. But then the driver did what most people would in that situation once they overcome their initial astonishment…he stomped on the brakes. Unfortunately, having nothing to grab on to, I was launched from the hood of the van into the air.

Flying

Soaring skyward without benefit of wires or vehicle (plane, kite, or glider) can be very freeing…at least at first. There's nothing holding you back, no restraints, not even gravity. But that feeling of freedom only lasts a moment, and then gravity does exert itself, and a sense of panic and impending doom take over.

I remember seeing the pavement approaching fast, causing me to think, "Oh boy, this is gonna hurt…" Moments later I landed with a hard whump. I slid across the tarmac, and the bits of gravel tore at me like teeth. There was a loud screeching sound (I think it was me), and then just grayness.

Vague shapes and colors faded in and out, and that horrendous caterwauling continued to fill the air making my head ache. A hand came out of the misty colors and touched me, but I felt nothing. Why, I wondered, can't I feel anything?

As I pondered that, I realized that my point of view had changed. I seemed to be watching everything from the side of the road. I was standing up, yet my body was still lying on the ground. I saw the driver of the van talking on his cell phone, and I realized that his passenger was the person leaning over me...or rather leaning over my body.

Several people from the golf course were rushing over to see what happened, and a lady from one of the nearby houses was saying something about not moving me.

But what captured my attention was the intensely bright column of white light shining out of the top of my body's head. It was mesmerizing.

I was spellbound by the glow. I really needed to touch it. I was compelled to touch it. Before I realized what I was doing, I had drifted over to where my body was. I reached out toward the light, and whoosh! I was sucked up the column of light like an envelope in a pneumatic mail tube.

The feeling of being pulled upward lasted seconds. Then there was a gentle calmness. I was suspended in that light. It was like being in the womb—timeless, weightless, and endless.

I drifted this way for an indeterminate length of time before I became aware of a vastness around me. The light no longer encapsulated just me. It had spread into an immense space with no topography; nothing you could call landscape. It was just a featureless limitlessness of white light. The only thing memorable about it was the emotional quality of it.

There was nothing frightening about it, nothing that would cause me a moment's hesitation about staying there. It might seem that an apparently sterile environment bathed in an intensely bright white light would be harsh or cold, but this was definitely not that. It was anything but hostile or austere; instead, it was serene and loving. As I stood there enjoying the wondrous joy of acceptance and love, the intensity of the love increased. Soon, I was swaddled in a blanket of tolerance, approval, and love.

There are no words for how I felt. I can try to explain how loving this place was, but words just can't do it justice. It was a place so filled with acceptance and love that you would never want to leave. I felt like I had finally come home; that I had finally found the one place where I fully belonged.

While I stood in awe, just relishing the marvelous kindness, acceptance, and love that surrounded me, I noticed a glow of golden light ahead of me in the distance. (Although I speak of time and distance, there really was no sense of either of them while I was there. Things simply were as they were when they were. It is only now, as I try to find words to describe things that I find I try to fit my experience into acceptable terms of time elapsed and space covered, but while experiencing this event, I had no feelings or sensations of distances or time.)

The golden light seemed to create a second area, an area beyond where I was in my white light. I felt an intense need to move toward that second, more golden light. The musical undertone that I had originally noticed, appeared to emanate from that golden area, and I so wanted to get closer to it.

As I moved toward that music, the loving acceptance grew stronger and my need to immerse myself in that golden light intensified. I came within steps of that golden border, yet was unable to advance any further.

In front of me hovered a being composed of little more than golden light. It stood exactly on the border between sections blocking me from advancing any further. Although humanoid in outline, there were few features other than large dark eyes and fingered hand-like appendages. It shimmered and vibrated in sync with the music coming from the golden area.

As we studied each other, a ball of blue-white light bounced through the air and hovered near my right shoulder. I felt that it was sentient, though I'm not sure how or why I came by that conclusion. I somehow just knew by looking at it that it was a thinking, living, creature. I also knew simply by looking at it, that it did not want me to go beyond the line where the two lights (white and gold) met. And neither did the golden man-creature.

Looking at these creatures, I became convinced that they were some sort of guardian or guide for this sacred place.

The golden being touched my shoulder, and my mind filled with images, colors, music, and words. Some of the message I readily understood. However, other parts seemed to slide past my conscious mind before I could comprehend the ideas or concepts.

At first, I worried that I wouldn't be able to comprehend and remember everything. The information came too fast and so many of the ideas were complex and would take time to process. But, the information flow paused, and I saw that none of the information was lost. It had simply slipped into my memory where I could recall it when I needed it. Only that which I would need in the immediate future was being held in my conscious mind.

The information flow continued for a few more moments, before changing. It went from a flow of more general knowing to a barrage of faces, of people I didn't know. Some of the faces appeared happy, while others appeared to be ailing or in pain.

The images shifted again, turning into scenes of individuals dying in fearful and lonely situations with no one to give them comfort and reassurance. Some of these people never found their way to the afterlife, while others did. But, instead, of finding love and acceptance when they arrived, these people were surrounded by nightmares, anger, darkness, and sadness.

Confronted with all that hurt and sorrow, I started crying. The tears streamed down my face, while the message continued. I was told that I could help people like them. I could ensure that everyone crossed over with understanding instead of fear; that I could be one of those designated to help people transition from physical life to spiritual life…but only if I wanted to.

I think I opened my mouth to ask some of the thousands of questions that now filled my brain. However, before I said a word, I heard, "All the answers to any questions you might have regarding this task are now within your grasp. You need only look inside yourself and the answers will be there."

I'm not sure what my face conveyed, but I felt confounded. I took a step forward but was blocked by the glowing orb. The golden being stepped back, and the glowing orb hovered in front of me. The orb touched my forehead, and a flow of music and images formed a picture that said, "You need to go now; it's not your time."

Disappointment filled me. To make me leave this place of love was so cruel. I wanted more than anything to join them; to learn how to sing and create the music with which they communicated. Most of all though, I wanted to remain in that cocoon of loving acceptance forever.

Again, the orb touched my forehead, and I heard, "Later…later, we promise."

Suddenly there was a horrible shrieking sound that pierced my head, and a man in a brown uniform was asking me questions—do I know what day of the week it is? Do I know my name? I stared at him uncomprehendingly. He asked again, and I answered slowly, unsure of where I was and what had happened. When I tried to sit up, the pain made me gasp, and the memory of the wild ride on the front of the van rushed back.

Other people in different uniforms surrounded me. I was poked, prodded, lifted, and strapped down. I couldn't move even had I wanted to. The man in brown finally stopped asking me questions, and I closed my eyes in relief. My eyelid was lifted and a moment later a light pierced my eyes. This made my head ache abominably, and I closed my eyes again.

There were lights and noises; echoes and shouting; and when I opened my eyes the sight of the ceiling rushing by made me dizzy. Once more I closed my eyes and tried to focus on what had just happened, or what I thought had just happened.

I knew I'd been in an accident; I had the aches and pains to prove it. But what I wasn't sure about was the whole other reality thing and the beings of light. Was that real or did I suffer some sort of hallucination?

As I tried to recall exactly what had happened in that fantastical other world, the more unreal it seemed. The most real aspect of it was the emotions that I had encountered and experienced. The emotions had been so real that I could feel my whole being light up just from the memories of the intensely positive and loving blanket of acceptance that had surrounded me there.

Recovery

THE HARDEST PART of the recovery wasn't just the physical pain, it was also the mental anguish. I was so disappointed at not being allowed to stay in that place of loving acceptance. I was convinced it meant I wasn't virtuous enough; that there was something missing in me, or not good enough about me.

It was my yoga instructor who gave me the phrase that helped me out of that particular funk. He started each session with some sort of inspirational quote, and this day his quote was from French philosopher, Pierre Teilhard de Chardin: "You are not a human being having a spiritual experience; you are a spiritual being having a human experience."

While I only half-heard most of his make-you-feel-good quotes, this one seemed to make it into my head and stick there. After class, I went about my day while his phrase continued to percolate in my brain.

It wasn't until the next morning, that I got it, though. Angry with myself for having to move so slowly due to my injuries and just plain tired of hurting all the time, I snapped at the physical therapist. Then, realizing what I had done, I burst into tears.

I hated myself for what I had said and how I had acted. This was the kind of behavior that had me convinced that I was hardly material worthy of being some sort of spiritual guru. How could I possibly be any kind of helper when I couldn't even help myself?

That's when the yoga teacher's quote really sunk in. Yes, I had been rude to my physical therapist. And yes, I owed her an apology. But didn't I owe myself an apology, too? After all, I was injured. I was in pain. And getting angry with myself or my therapist was a foolish waste of energy. We were both human, and there was nothing wrong with that.

I wasn't perfect; no one was. I wasn't above being angry, sad, happy, or experiencing pain. I was HUMAN. Before I could develop compassion for anyone else, I needed to be compassionate to myself. I needed to accept myself for who and what I was— flaws and all. Because once I understood that I wasn't perfect, I could accept others for what and who they were, too.

Once I recognized that, I began to work toward accepting myself and others. It was a struggle, especially on those days when my impatience reared up and started wreaking havoc with my attitude. And I was constantly running into situations guaranteed to push my impatience button. Situations like the need-to-be-someplace-but-can't-get-the-traffic-to-move situation, or the I-just-need-one-thing-but-there's-a-mile-long-line-at-checkout, and similar situations.

I've always said that if you find yourself in similar situations repeatedly, it's because there's something you're just not getting; there's something you're not accepting or understanding. Based on my own situations, I soon recognized that maybe I had a few more lessons to learn and a few more experiences to have as a physical being.

Impatience may seem like a trivial issue; but trust me, it can be a raging beast. When impatience runs loose, the words and emotions that spill out can (and do) push everyone near you away. I'm still working to tame the beast; however, it's a chameleon. Just when I think I have it identified, it sprouts a new set of horns, another tail, or larger set of fangs.

During this recovery period, I also found that my impatience was a great humbler. Whenever I started to think of myself as more aware than the next guy, of having evolved further (spiritually) than everyone else, that ol' impatience kicked in. It would show me quite quickly that I was no better than anyone else.

So, it was a challenging time on many levels.

Struggling

ANOTHER ISSUE I was struggling with was my growing doubt as to the reality of the experience. As time moved forward and my body healed, I grew more doubtful of what I had experienced. After all, I had taken a pretty hard blow to the head. Who knows what type of delusions a knock like that can cause.

I so wanted that experience to be real, though. The emotional impact of that experience had been so intense that even just thinking about it, I could still feel the cocoon of warmth and love that had surrounded me there. Those memories filled me with hope and positivity; two things I really needed as I continued my struggle to recover.

However, I had always been all about the logic of life. I loved procedures, science, and law because they followed rational progressive patterns. Therefore, my rational side dictated that what I had experienced was probably a result of my head colliding with the pavement.

Basically, it was heart versus head, and the struggle was exhausting. What I hadn't yet grasped was that the struggle was actually love (heart) versus fear (mind).

While my inner voice was assuring me that it was all good; that it was something I wanted and needed to do, my fear (what I called logic) was trying to convince me how foolish I would end up looking, how ridiculous the whole idea of an afterlife guide was, and asking me why the heck anyone up there would want my help.

Although, I did believe in reincarnation and some type of afterlife, my idea of an afterlife was vague. It didn't contain angels, celestial choirs, or golden gates with long bearded gate keepers. So, I began to question my vision of a golden being that looked more space alien than angelic, and a light globe that didn't fit into any type of religious afterlife story that I had ever heard.

I was raised in a Christian society; however, my family was more agnostic than Christian. I read about and visited with people who participated in or belonged to diverse types of religious institutions. I even attended services at different religious affiliations.

However, when it came down to it, I was more spiritual than religious. I believed in something more than us. I believed in a stopping off place where you waited until you incarnated into another person (I don't subscribe to the incarnating as animals or bugs—people only). And I believed in a holistic view of the world—hurt a butterfly and it might cause a war since all creatures are connected at an intrinsic level.

So, while this whole dead-but-alive experience fit within my world view in some ways, it was totally skewed. I was constantly bouncing back and forth between accepting the experience and thinking myself nuts for even considering the veracity of it.

But what if it were real, did that make me a lunatic? And if it weren't real, what did that mean for everyone when they died? Did that mean that all those people who said that there was nothing beyond this one life were right? That was something I couldn't accept. There had to be more to us than just this physical shell. I couldn't buy into the theory that we were simply an accident of biology.

It was no wonder that I spent several months alternating between anger, depression, hope, and happiness. I became bogged down in my own inner turmoil. I was unable to focus on anything, and because of that my physical recovery suffered.

On days when I believed in myself and my sanity, I went to my therapy sessions and did my exercises. But on those days of doubt, I was angry, truculent, and argumentative.

Eventually, I became convinced that logic and rationality were right. Because, just like that little devil that sits on your shoulder, they fed my self-doubt and my fear. This constant influx of negativity made it hard to hear the small, inner voice that kept whispering to me that the love was real; that the need for my help was real.

When that inner voice did get through, it wasn't strong enough to break negativity's hold. Instead, it just triggered an inner conflict as I fought with myself over what I should believe or do.

Rationality and logic love fear, and for most of us, fear is easier to accept than love. And so it was for me. While I was busy making lists of pros and cons, rationality and logic were in heaven. But the moment I began to listen to that tiny voice of instinct and emotion, they fired off the guns of doubt and anguish shooting down every positive thought or idea.

It wasn't until I returned to my meditations that I finally managed to drown out that negativity enough to hear what love had to say. It's a softer voice, but once you tune into it, it's amazing. The affection, the gentle echoes of encouragement, and the strong feelings of self-assurance that your inner voice offers can be immensely helpful.

However, even while hearing that calming voice of encouragement and love urging me forward, there remained a niggling kernel of doubt.

I worked in the financial world—a world of narrow minds, polished images, and insular lives. That meant that most of my acquaintances and pals also had narrow views of the world, views that weren't really wide enough to encompass anything beyond this reality. They seemingly only believed in increasing their bottom lines and gaining as much "treasure" as possible.

I had some friends that (I thought) might believe me, but I was still too full of doubt over the reality of it all to risk losing them. So, the great debate continued: should I dare share this story with anyone? Would anyone believe me? Or would I lose everything—friends, job, family if I tried to tell them?

Should I Share My Story?

I CAN'T REMEMBER how many times I tried to broach the subject of what had happened with someone, anyone. But every time I got close, I backed away. I would start to say something, but then clam up, convinced that the person wouldn't believe me.

Sometimes, just the thought of telling someone had me in a cold sweat. I would imagine the look of total disbelief on their face, and my insides turned icy and my stomach knotted up.

A month after I returned to work, I went to lunch with my best friend, someone who had known me for years. She knew all my strange quirks, or most of them, anyway. She'd experienced first-hand some of my idiosyncrasies, such as knowing things I had no way of knowing. So, I convinced myself that telling her about my experience was the best thing to do.

Once seated in the restaurant, she gave me the perfect opening, too, when she asked me how I was doing and whether I was having bad dreams or emotional issues from the accident. But instead of using that as my lead into what I was struggling with, I gave her my usual,

"I'm fine," and turned the conversation to some other topic.

We finished our lunch after having touched on a dozen or more topics, but I left feeling more down than I had in a month.

I couldn't get over the fact that I had somehow betrayed her friendship. She had accepted a lot of weirdness from me over the years, but without even giving her a chance, I decided she wouldn't be willing to accept this. Who was I to make that decision for her?

That question led me to wonder even more about my decision to stay silent. After all, my family and closest friends had all put up with a lot of bizarreness from me, what was one more bit of oddness?

I'm what most of the world calls *intuitive*. I can sometimes catch glimpses of major events before they happen, but mostly I know smaller (more local) things. For instance, I usually know who's calling right before the phone rings; I tend to finish other people's sentences for them; and sometimes, I find myself humming a tune that someone else is thinking about. There are also the occasional precognitive flashes like the one I had about my father and his promotion.

My father was a member of the local police department, and at one point he was contemplating taking the exam needed to get promoted. I remember having a vision of my father decked out in his uniform while surrounded by other members of the department all equally dressed up.

He was looking immensely proud and had a broad smile on his face. Then an older man in a uniform with lots of braid on the shoulders handed my father an official looking document. The whole vision was filled with a sense of pomp and circumstance, and the letters SGT kept buzzing through my mind.

About a month later, my dad announced that his captain had selected him to take the sergeant's exam. I told my dad that he would do great, and he simply gave me an indulgent smile. He knew that I had no idea how difficult the exam was, but then my dad didn't know what I did, either—that I had already seen him being awarded the promotion. My father did do great, and he received recognition of his accomplishment in a ceremony just like the one I had seen.

And because I've demonstrated these idiosyncrasies often enough, the people closest to me just accept that that's the way I am. I just wasn't sure if they'd be willing to accept this latest bit of strangeness.

Why Me?

ALSO LURKING SOMEWHERE in the back of my mind, was the question I didn't want to look too closely at. Yet, during my recovery there would be odd little moments when the question would surface. It was especially prone to creeping into my thoughts during those instances of increased self-doubt. Each time the question popped up, though, I pushed it away.

At nights, the question was like a pesky mosquito…noisy, persistent, and impossible to squash. So, instead of sinking into the land of dreams, I was tormented by the constant reiterative drubbing of the question flitting through my brain: Why me? Why choose me?

When I wasn't in physical therapy, I was doing research. I had decided to find any information that might explain what had happened to me.

I'm a researcher and bibliophile by nature. I tend to think like Hermione in the Harry Potter books that all answers can be found in a book. So, I spent a great deal of time pouring over books, magazines, and esoteric texts only found in those often musty, half-forgotten places called libraries. I also spent a lot of

time sifting through the Internet's multitude of
medical, metaphysical, and spiritual web sites.

As I sifted through some of the more bizarre Internet
sites, I found several websites that seemed promising.
They presented accounts from people who'd had
experiences like my own. These sites even had a name
for these experiences. They called them near-death
experiences or NDEs.

I wasn't sure I had been near death at any time during
the accident, but the descriptions of what constituted
an NDE certainly fit what I had experienced.

It's Called an NDE

ONCE I KNEW what it was called, I went to the library and checked out all the books and magazine articles that they had about it. I even read through the reports of those who claimed it was a physiological response to oxygen deprivation and not a spiritual experience.

The more I read about NDEs, the more comfortable I was in accepting my own experience as something real. Whether the experience was spiritual or physiological wasn't as important (at that moment) as knowing it wasn't something caused by a malfunction of my mental processes. (In other words, I wasn't nuts.)

One of the websites I referenced was run by a group of physicians. As their patients reported these near-death experiences to them, they decided to create a forum for other people to share their own experiences. It was a place where people could report their experiences without the fear of being doubted, trolled, or considered foolish. These doctors even provided a type of questionnaire to help everyone compile and organize their thoughts into a more cohesive and logical flow.

As I debated whether I wanted to log my experience with them or not, I read through the questionnaire. It was rather straight forward: describe the incident that caused the NDE; describe the NDE itself; have you ever experienced anything similar…my first response was to mentally say "no, of course not." But then I remembered a sailing accident I'd had when I was in my early twenties.

It was a picture-perfect summer day. A gentle breeze was blowing, the sky was like a Monet painting with gentle blues and turquoises mingled with the wispy whites of clouds.

Lake Michigan was calm, with only a few gently rocking waves, and standing on the dock in the marina, we could see a smattering of colorful sails dotting the horizon.

It was too nice of a day to go into work, so my friend and I went to the marina where he had a small two-sail dinghy. Ignoring the need for life jackets, we untied the boat and headed out to enjoy the day.

The wind caught the sails and we raced out beyond the breakwater and up the coast toward Saugatuck Harbor. The sun reddened our shoulders and our noses, and the wind tangled our hair, but we didn't care. Our smiles were huge and our sense of freedom profound.

Flying across the water on this little piece of fiberglass was as close to heaven as we could imagine. When you looked out across the water, away from the shore, you could almost visualize yourself as being the only person left in the world. You, the sun, the water, and the wind. It was marvelous.

Halfway along our journey, we saw the sky ahead of us turning gray and gloomy. The clouds had become an angry gang of bullies, threatening and overbearing. They blotted out the sun and the wind had turned nasty and blustery.

Several streaks of lightning burst across the sky. The waves slapped at the boat like a hand slamming into a tabletop. What had started out as a fun way to skive off work, had now become a challenging misadventure, instead. As the sky scowled and the wind bit at us, the water became even more turbulent and hard-edged.

Hoping to avoid the worst of the storm, we decided to return to our originating port. However, as we turned the boat, something went wrong. Tacking through the turn, the sail luffed. But when we attempted to rein it in the wind gusted unexpectedly and snagged the sail. It jerked the boat sideways, pitching both of us into the water and turtling the boat.

My friend swam clear of the boat; however, I became tangled in the lines and was unable to free myself. As panic set in, I struggled harder, tangling myself even more. I could no longer tell if I was angled up or down. The water all looked the same. My lungs burned, and I knew I wasn't going to make it.

One minute my chest was aching, and the next I was floating calmly in the water. It was about then that I saw the brilliant patch of white light shining just beyond my reach. The light was so bright that it blocked out everything else.

That light appeared so inviting that I wanted to touch it, to place myself within its glow. I remember reaching my hand toward it, but I didn't have the strength to push myself forward to where it was.

I floated, drifting with the currents; then nothing.

The next thing I remembered I was coughing up water on the deck of someone's boat. Another boater had seen our craft go over and had managed to pull me on board.

I hadn't thought about that event in years, but now I wondered if that white light was related to the light I had entered following the bike-versus-car accident. According to all the research I had done, the boating accident wasn't a classic NDE; however, there were others who had written about incomplete experiences like that one.

Being Out of Body

AS I CONTINUED to research NDEs, I discovered that experiencing an out of body event during the NDE was quite common. This information triggered a bit of reflection regarding my own life, specifically my childhood.

There had been some very odd occurrences when I was growing up. And my path through life hadn't been the straightest. I had followed a lot of challenging, yet interesting paths to get to where I was now.

I had stumbled upon one such curiously crooked path when I was young. It was a path that led me to learn how to leave my body.

OBEs, What are They?

Out of Body Experiences (OBEs) occur when you shift your focus from the physical to the astral. By shifting your awareness from the physical plane, you release your spiritual energy so that it is no longer restricted to the confines of your body.

Studies of the mind have identified a specific region of the brain associated with spatial recognition. In other words, there is a part of your brain that helps you fix yourself within a specific time and space; it helps you retain a sense of self by enabling you to identify your location as being within your own body.

However, some people can control that aspect of their brain, and can turn it off and on at will. With it turned off, a person can identify with a larger venue; their awareness is able to expand outward beyond the confines of their body. Also, with it off, a person can travel to remote locations and report what they observe.

These studies have used MRI's and brain scans during the travel and viewing experiments, which have shown the parts of the brains that were triggered. Each time the participant claimed to have launched themselves free of their bodies, the spatial recognition area of their brains was shown in the MRI to have been shut down; and it didn't come back on until the participants returned.

While the subject in the experiment traveled, various other portions of their mind were triggered, such as the visual cortex, even though the physical body had its eyes closed. The scientists conducting these studies claim this shows that something real is happening and that while the body remains fixed in place, the mind (and perhaps more than the mind) has traveled somewhere else.

Some scientists say that this proves that a person's true awareness spans multiple realities and multiple planes yet is limited by the physical body. Since most of us rarely focus on anything other than our immediate world…the physical world, all we know is the body we wear and the surroundings we exist in while being the person we are. If, however, we shift our focus (our awareness) to that part of us not confined within our body, we will be able to walk free of our physical restraints.

This spatial recognition center also helps each of us relate to and understand the concept of time, as well as space. Therefore, when this center is turned off, our perception of time becomes skewed. So, when we go out of body, we may only be away from our bodies a few moments, but it can seem like hours.

While this may appear to be a minor inconvenience, it can become quite deadly. If you remain detached from the physical world for too long, the health of your physical body could be compromised.

Most people who have reported having OBEs fit into two classifications: those who seek the experience, and those whose experiences are spontaneous. Of those in the latter category, most said that they experienced the out of body moment during some traumatic event, such as a car accident, a fall, or some equally emotionally painful situation. In fact, in 1974, scientists suggested that: "…OBEs were a stress reaction to either a physically or emotionally painful situation."

My Own OBEs

All my life, I tended to avoid extremely painful
incidents by leaving. Some call it *transcending the
pain*, others call it *walking out*, but mostly it's just
referred to as being *out of body*. In fact, the first time I
found myself outside of my physical body was when I
broke my arm.

I was about five or six years old and riding in the
backseat of the family car, my mother was driving. We
were stopped at a stop light and I was staring out the
side window. I noticed a lady in a big dark sedan pull
out of the parking lot; her car was aimed right at where
I was sitting. I just knew that she was going to hit our
car, but before I could say anything to my mother, I
was somewhere else.

When I looked around, I was in the backseat of
another car and a strange lady was staring into her
rear-view mirror apparently as shocked to see me as I
was to see her. I screamed at her that I wanted my
mother, and the next moment I was standing in the
street next to where the two cars were crunched
together staring in the window at myself.

The confusion of being both in the car and outside of
the car shocked me, and I felt pulled towards the me
inside the car. A moment later I was in the backseat of
the family car holding my arm to my chest and crying
because it hurt so much.

That incident frightened me while it was happening, but it also intrigued me. I remember spending almost an entire year trying to find a way to make it happen again. I kept wishing myself to be ghost-like just as I had been before, but no amount of wishing made it so.

It wasn't until I roller skated down three flights of steps that I managed to be ghost-like again. (I have subsequently learned that roller skating is best done on flat surfaces.)

Then, just like the first time, it was a matter of avoiding consequences. In this case, the consequence of my body's colliding with the floor at the bottom of the stairs. Rather than put me off, though, this experience only increased my desire to find a way to walk free of my body, but without the threat (and reality) of extreme pain.

Even as a youngster I was rather bookish, and my fascination with psychic phenomenon just gave me more impetus for spending time in the library. From what I learned, Fakirs and Yogis claimed that psychic powers (of which walking free of the body was considered one) could be heightened and refined through meditation. So, I began to study different meditation and breathing techniques in the hopes of recreating the out of body experience (without the pain.)

In my 'tween years I finally managed a deep enough meditation that it allowed me to step free of my body at will. The first time I did so, I remember gazing down at my body lying quietly on the neatly made bed, and then ghosting through the closed door to the hallway of my family's home. I wandered from room to room, slipping through walls and doors.

Sliding through the house like a ghost was fun, yet disconcerting. The first few times I did it, I was frightened that I would become embedded in the walls, unable to free myself. Yet I didn't want to quit because the I felt so free and exhilarated.

Because of my fear, I usually kept my out of body experiences short (usually less than thirty minutes). However, after a dozen or so experiences, I grew braver. Determined to see just how much I could do and just how far I could travel, I pulled myself free of my body for another try.

This time when I walked away from my body, I heard the radio coming from the kitchen. Instead of ghosting downstairs, though, I thought hard about being in the kitchen where the music was. And suddenly I was.

My mother was at the counter chopping vegetables for a stew. I tried to grab a piece of carrot, but, like a wraith, my hand went right past the carrot slices. I also tried to make my mother notice me; however, no amount of shouting or waving of hands and arms made her aware of my presence.

I concentrated on the orchard behind our house, and poof, I was there. This was marvelous. I thought about the playground near the school and popped myself over there. Then I popped over to the library, and a dozen other of my favorite places. It was fantastic. I could go anywhere I wanted just by thinking about it.

A sense of weakness overcame me, and I felt a strong urge to return to the bedroom where my body was. I let that urge pull me along, and gliding through the house like an apparition, I floated upstairs and fell back into place. That's precisely what it felt like, too...falling.

My ghost-self plopped back into place, and a restored me jerked up from the bed and looked around. When I spotted the clock on the bedside table, I was flabbergasted. Several hours had elapsed, yet it had seemed like mere moments while I was popping from place to place sans body.

The more I explored and experimented with being out of body, the more I came to understand that time wasn't a constant. While I understood one minute to be 60 seconds, when I was in a non-physical state that same 60 seconds stretched like taffy.

It's only recently that I learned about the spatial/time center in our brains. Back then, all I knew was that when I stepped outside of my body, I no longer experienced time the same way. My perception of time and space was skewed, and it was much too easy to underestimate how long I had been away.

And if I crossed into the astral realm, time truly seemed to stand still. I now know it's because time, or our understanding of the concept, doesn't apply anywhere but in the physical world. The further away from the physical world we go, the more difficult it is to maintain the concept of time and that sense of time passing. However, back then, I only knew that I had to be extra careful when wandering away from my body.

Luckily, I found other ways of making sure I never stayed out too long (such as an alarm clock next to the body). I discovered that when I signaled the body, the signal found me via the connection I had with my body. Therefore, I could set the alarm to go off after an hour, ensuring that I never stayed away too long.

It All Leads Back to Here

AFTER MY BIKE accident, I continued researching OBEs and NDEs. This led me to reviewing my own life and some of the paths I had ended up following.

My path through life may not have been the most direct. There had been times when I wondered about some of my choices and where they would lead; but now I had a better overall view of things. (Isn't that always the way? I've always heard that hindsight is clearer than foresight.)

I now saw my questionable choices in a different light. For instance, the reasons for choosing to be an intuitive, and the reasons for selecting the family that I had, now made perfect sense. Even the choices I made to involve myself with certain people or situations seemed more understandable now.

I had always wanted to teach, and I now understood that I had. Although I hadn't been a teacher in the traditional sense, I had still instructed people about love, enlightenment, philosophy, and awareness. Instead of schoolbooks and classrooms, I had used my newsletters, blogs, and assorted writings.

I'd even held group meditation sessions so that other people could experience the freedom of being out of body or the feelings of oneness that I felt when I meditated. However, now it seemed that I had a chance to take everything I had learned about the cycle of life, death, and the afterlife, and share it with others in my own unique way.

I had always understood that every choice we made helped us in our life's goal, but sometimes it's hard to see just exactly what that goal is. We all become so immured in our everyday lives that it's not easy to see the overarching picture. But that picture was much clearer to me now.

All my choices had helped me become more accepting of events and people. They helped me look beneath the surface of life and see that there is so much more to it. There's a whole breadth of life beyond this physical plane, but most people never know about it, not until they die, anyway.

But I could help them understand, and along the way I could learn more, too. For me, that's always the most fun—learning—and I find I learn the most when information is shared with others. Not everyone sees life (or death) in the same terms that I do, so I find it quite informative to see how others interpret or understand things based on their different points of view.

I now realized that my choices to study metaphysics, psychology, theoretical and quantum physics, along with the different religious, spiritual, and philosophical ideas and ideologies had only been small steps along a larger path. This larger path was one that I had started several lifetimes ago and was still traveling. It seemed that I was again going to stride down this path of helping and learning, and I couldn't wait.

Once I decided that the events were real, I sat down and wrote out all the questions I had (I love my lists); for instance, why would anyone (especially some sort of spiritual guide) think I was qualified to help people transition from life to death? And how do you escort or guide someone to the afterlife if you're still alive? What does it take to transition someone? And what does transitioning someone really mean?

It made me feel better to have the questions written up. However, once I had them all listed, I had to add one more: How do you contact a being of light (or was it an angel?) to let them know you need to talk with them?

Accepting the Job

I WONDERED HOW I was supposed to let the beings of light know that I wanted to speak with them again. I thought about saying a prayer, but again I didn't know who to direct it to. Did angels have names, and if so, why didn't the being I spoke with give me his (or was that hers)?

I had no idea how many beings of light or angels there were. Would my message get passed along if I sent it to the wrong being?

I know I was being too literal, thinking like a human being. But, then again, that's what I was.

I needn't have worried, though. Apparently, these beings are adept at tuning in and responding to us when necessary.

For me, the responses came in a series of dreams. The dreams didn't answer my questions with literal images. Instead, in their imagery I found the keys to unlock the embedded information from my initial meeting with the light beings—the information that I had stored for later recall.

The beings must have sensed my acceptance of their proposal. Because on the fifth night, instead of just sending dreams, they all came in person.

Welcome Home

I had gone to bed like any other night and was soon asleep. Suddenly, a bright light filled the bedroom. I groaned and thought that it couldn't possibly be time to get up yet since I was sure I had only just gone to bed a couple of hours ago.

I rolled toward the light and tried to open my eyes. However, the light was so intense that I had to squeeze my eyes into slits as I searched for the cause of this unnatural brilliance.

As I scanned past the bedroom doorway, I saw a group of people in silhouette standing in the hall just outside the bedroom. The brilliantly shining light seemed to be coming from behind them, backlighting them and making it impossible to see them clearly.

Almost as if they could tell I was looking at them, the glow that surrounded them receded. Now the only glow was around the white shirt, pants, and shoes that they all wore. It was like they were standing under a giant black light or, perhaps, they were wearing glow-in-the-dark clothing.

Sitting up, I rubbed at my eyes, and peered closer. There were maybe 10 to 12 of them standing half in the bedroom and half in the hallway beyond. They all looked like ice cream vendors in their glowing white outfits.

I've had some bizarre dreams, and some of them have seemed awfully real, but I'd never experienced anything like this.

Completely convinced that I was in some wild and crazy dream sequence (probably brought on by a midnight craving for ice cream), I dropped back onto the bed. I rolled over with my back to these strange glowing apparitions and tried to go back to sleep.

The light flared again. This time the room was so lit up, it was like being in the sun itself. I pushed myself upright and tried to glare at the group. However, it's hard to glare at someone when you're squinting.

If you wake up my husband... I started to think, and huge smiles covered all their faces. I looked down at my husband. He was sleeping more soundly than a baby, something I wished I were doing. A smile curved his lips, and his mild snores filled the room.

I turned toward my nighttime interrupters who had once again dimmed their glow. They continued smiling at me, though, and in my mind, I felt their messages of welcome and acceptance.

Their smiles were contagious, and I couldn't help but smile back. They held out their arms toward me, and I somehow knew what they wanted me to do. I let go and stepped out of my body, which sprawled back onto the bed.

As I glided across the bedroom toward the group, I looked down and realized that I was now dressed identically to them. So, wearing my ice cream vendor outfit, I flowed into the warm welcoming glow that they all emanated.

With the entire group surrounding me, the glow from our combined spirits was almost too bright to endure. Yet I basked in the reassuring calm and loving acceptance that they imparted.

I had the feeling that I knew them all; like they were part of some extended family I had forgotten about. Yet, when I studied their faces none of them were familiar. However, as I met the eyes of several of them there was an instant of recognition. I knew them, yet I didn't. I knew them in their spiritual forms, but not in their earthly forms.

An older-looking man whose face I only vaguely recognized, but whose soul I definitely knew, held out his hand. When I took it, my mind was flooded with information. It came in the form of words, pictures, feelings, and music. It was like a tidal wave of memories washing over me. Concepts, ideas, and knowledge that I had always known but had not remembered, were no longer hidden from me. I smiled at RJ (I now knew his name, which had been part of the information transmitted to me) and looked around at the rest of the group.

I knew that some of the group had known each other for a long time; while others, had only been part of the group for a few decades. Those I recognized, were souls that I had interacted with at other times—it might have been during one or more lifetimes spent on Earth or it might have been during some between times on the astral plane.

The members of the group who appeared rather androgynous, were souls that had never incarnated; therefore, they chose very generic looks. The other members of the group chose appearances similar to what they looked like in their current lives or their lives just completed (for those who were no longer physical).

I looked back to RJ, the man whose hand I held. He was one of those I had spent several lifetimes with. He had also been my astral plane instructor for several lifetimes. He was the one who had most helped me to prepare for the task of escorting the dead.

As a guide and an instructor, he was without a presence in the physical world. Guides exist only in the astral world. They have either never incarnated in physical form, or they have finished their physical lives and lessons, so choose to remain in the astral plane.

Guides work with people like me because we want to be guides "when we grow up." And, apparently, I had spent several lifetimes already learning how to do this job (mostly through observation of and instruction from RJ). Now, it was time to put that training to use. Of course, since escorts (like me) still maintain a presence in the physical world, we can only work part time, but then that's probably why there are quite a few of us.

I gazed back at the group surrounding me and I understood that this group was to be *my crew*. We would be working together (sometimes as a group, sometimes in pairs, and other times as individuals) to help people transition from life to afterlife. They had come tonight to welcome me home.

We all lose our memories when we're born. It's how we participate in life. As we go through each life, though, we regain some of those memories. We call it enlightenment, or expanded awareness, but it's basically just remembering. So, when I had taken on this physical life, I had forgotten about all these extracurricular activities that I used to do and a lot of the earlier training that I had received. However, now it was time to remember, and my crew was going to help me do that. It might take me several sessions with them, but that was okay, we had the time.

Meanwhile, the circle of hands that had begun with me and RJ, closed, and a moment later we were all standing in the gray, foggy nothingness of the transition level. This is the level of the astral plane nearest the physical plane. It's the easiest area reached, and many a lost soul and dreamer has found themselves here at one time or another.

We dropped hands and I looked around, a question forming in my mind as to what was going on. Before the question was even half-formed, one of the crew signaled me to be patient. I nodded, as the realization hit me that we were all connected here in the astral plane.

While the emotions and directed thoughts of those in my crew were the easiest to perceive, if I focused, I could also hear others in the background. Not every thought was transmitted (that would be noisy indeed), but those thoughts that you would normally verbalize could be read by those you were going to speak to. So, instead of having to ask the question out loud for it to be heard, this member of my crew responded to my question, which he heard, based on my intention to ask.

A moment later, the gray mist swirled and began to shift. It whirled around my feet, and then the mist rose up in a column where it solidified and became a pillar of white stone. All around me arose other pillars, and then a ceiling appeared filled with stars. Soon we were standing in a huge coliseum-like structure.

When I looked around, I saw other groups like ours gathered in this large arena. Some groups were dressed like us, others were in white robes, and still others wore toga-like apparel. Within minutes the huge edifice was crowded as more and more groups appeared.

Soon, I felt more than heard a low thrumming hum. It

seemed to come from nowhere and everywhere. This was followed by a growing golden glow that appeared in the center of this room full of white light. The golden light continued to emerge, and everyone sort of fell back a step or two, creating a circle two and three layers deep as the golden light intensified and grew larger.

The thrum grew more noticeable, growing in intensity until my entire being vibrated with it. It flowed through me like a chorus of heavenly voices, yet it seemed also to be filled with bells, but was also an orchestration played with such beauty and passion that I felt myself weeping.

Without even realizing it, we had all begun to hold hands, and now we were all connected, one with the other. The golden glow filled the building overpowering our simple white light, and I saw the rapture on the faces around me.

Joy and love surrounded us, and I couldn't stop smiling. The moment seemed to last for hours, yet when it was over, I thought it had ended too soon. I looked around as the music faded and saw smiles and tears everywhere. I reached out to hug the person/soul next to me and knew I had made the right choice for me. It was good to be back.

I awoke the next morning still feeling the ecstasy of my late-night experience and the joy of returning to my job.

Astral Plane Career Paths

THE JOB I was accepting was one I had spent several lifetimes studying for, but only after I had experimented with at least one other possible career path.

I'm sure there are as many types of careers or jobs in the astral plane as there are in the physical plane; however, I only know about two of them. That's because I was interested in them, so had checked them out. Those two career paths are:

- Guardians
- Guides

It's the guides' path that I've decided to pursue, but who knows…in a millennium or so, I might decide to change and see what it's like to be a guardian.

What is the Guardian Career Path?

I checked out the guardian career path before deciding on my current career path. And while I found the Guardian career path fascinating, I decided it wasn't the one for me (at least not this time). However, this is what I remember about that career path.

Guardian Career Job Titles	Description
Watcher	Usually a corporeal being who observes and watches a small section of physical reality for anomalies.
Guardian	Usually a non-corporeal being who helps and guides people. They are often referred to as Guardian Angels.
Advisor	A non-corporeal being who helps you during your between life periods. They help you do life lesson reviews or make choices for your next incarnation.
Monitor	A non-corporeal being who acts as a "supervisor" to watchers and guardians.
Oversoul	A non-corporeal collective of souls that keeps watch over everything. They understand the interconnectedness of all the realities and all things (sentient and non-sentient).

The entry level position for this career path is watcher. Like escorts (the job I was taking on), those who function as watchers are corporeal yet working on the astral plane.

Watchers spend much of their time doing what their title suggests…watching. Each watcher is assigned to a specific reality of the physical world (a specific time and place, such as a reality where the Viet Nam War never occurred, or Napoleon didn't lose at Waterloo). They're also assigned to a specific group or type of group (such as a group of people, group of animals, group of insects, etc.). They then spend their time in the lowest level of the astral plane (the transition level) and observe this group. If something not accounted for begins to occur, they can step in and take the appropriate action, or they can call for a guardian.

The appropriate action can be anything or nothing (no action other than to make a note or notify an escort or guide that someone is coming or going and will need assistance), or they can make the necessary modifications (those they have the authority to make) to keep reality humming along.

For instance, in our Earth reality, all trees have a basic structure—trunk, branches, leaves or needles. We all expect that. Sometimes anomalies can cause our reality to flicker, the way a storm might cause our electricity to surge or stop and our lights to flicker in our houses. If this happens, then a watcher or guardian needs to step in to make sure that our reality continues to look and feel the way it should. No one wants you to come along and see a tree that looks like something out of a cartoon with bubble gum leaves and metal branches. Talk about a mind-bending experience. So, watchers try to keep things as normal as possible.

Guardians are those souls who dwell on the astral plane. They have no physical presence (normally). While watchers can stabilize reality and keep things functioning the way they should, guardians can step in and adjust lives. Perhaps you overslept by five minutes. But because of that you're now rushing and so don't notice the car running the red light as you're crossing the street.

A guardian (sometimes called a guardian angel) might *adjust* things to make sure that the car misses you or at least doesn't kill you. They have that power. However, they also have the responsibility to ensure that they don't interfere with your choices. So, they walk a pretty narrow line between what they can and what they should do. After all, it is your life; they're just there to help.

Advisors primarily work in the decisions level of the astral plane. They help you determine what reality you might want to incarnate into so that you can complete certain life goals and objectives. They know the intricacies of all the available timelines and different realities, so can easily point you in the best direction for your next life.

Monitors and oversouls work hand-in-hand to keep everything working as it should. Oversouls are a soul collective. They are a blending of souls; a merging of souls from the integration level of the astral plane who, once integrated, continue their learning by helping to keep all parts of every reality functioning the way it should, the way that the souls within the reality expect it to.

If you think of Earth as a large Broadway play, then the watcher is the set director, the guardian the stage director, the monitor is the theatre director, and the oversoul is the managing director. Each has their role to play, and each has a different level of involvement.

Oversouls keep watch over everything—the planet, the animals, the plants, the different time streams (realities), and they also create different realities based on choices that people, countries, and worlds make. They understand the interconnectedness of all the realities and all things (sentient and non-sentient).

Monitors focus on just one aspect of the whole, such as canines, or felines, or trees, or mountains. In a business structure, they would be the department head to the oversouls' role of senior VP, while the guardians are the line managers.

Monitors are responsible for keeping their portion of physical reality functioning smoothly; keeping it functioning in the expected way (expected by those who are incarnate in that particular reality). So, if they're in charge of dogs, they make sure that all dogs have the same basic structure, the same basic responses, and the same dog-like mannerisms.

I Chose the Guide Career Path

The path I decided to follow was one that would lead toward a sort of professorship on the astral plane.

Guide Career Job Titles	Description
Escort	Usually a corporeal being who helps others transcend the realities.
Guide	Usually a non-corporeal being who helps with births, deaths, agreements, and life re-enactments.
Counselor	A non-corporeal being who provides insight and advice either one-on-one or to large groups of souls.
Instructor	A non-corporeal being who offers training, information, and insight on assorted topics to any soul who wishes to join one of their "classes."
Master	A non-corporeal collective of souls that offers their wisdom and insight to anyone (corporeal or non-corporeal) who asks them.

On the career path I chose, the escort is the corporeal transcender who works on the astral plane. Escorts help travelers and visitors to the astral plane, and they help those who are transitioning between life and afterlife.

Once an escort transitions from the physical world to the astral world, they can become guides. As they progress in their learning and their experiences, they can move on to be counselors.

Counselors help other souls decide whether to move forward to the next plane of existence, stay at the astral plane level, or return to the physical plane. They provide insight and advice. As they become proficient and adept in this role, they can move on to become instructors...sort of a super teacher.

Instructors can help a single soul from one level to the next, walking them through the entire experience until that soul decides to go back to the physical world or move on to the next plane, or the instructor can monitor and help other guides and escorts. In other words, they have a wider set of choices because they have gained more experiences than those of us who are guides and escorts. They also "teach classes" on a wide variety of topics.

From instructor, the next step is master. The masters are a collective of souls (like the oversoul). This group of souls has progressed from escort, to guide, to guardian, and have now integrated their energies and knowledge with other souls to create a single entity. They offer insights, classes, and information to anyone who asks for it (whether that person is corporeal or non-corporeal).

Of course, the guide and guardian career paths are only two of the career paths available and not every soul needs to follow either of them. There are countless other options, including just doing nothing (except perhaps playing golf and hanging about). It's up to each of us to decide what we want to do.

For me, I was going to pick up where I had left off. I was going back to being an escort.

Learning the Ropes

Over the next few weeks my nights were remarkably busy. I became a regular visitor to the astral plane. Being there helped me remember all that I had already learned, which was important if I wanted to get on with my next set of lessons.

It took about a dozen visits before I remembered everything, including the many nuances of manipulating astral energy.

To help me remember and relearn, I attended lectures by the masters. Different masters would offer information, insights, and instructions to groups of souls wanting to learn. There was no schedule posted for these events; instead, I just seemed to know when and where to be, and voila. I and dozens of others would be in a congenial setting listening to these wonderfully loving souls impart their wisdom.

As I listened, information that I had known, but repressed, filtered to the forefront of my mind. It made me realize that I had been living my whole life for this. All my efforts to learn how to transition from the physical world to the astral world, all my studying of esoteric subjects, and my need to see beyond the reality of our world and understand how everything really works, now made sense. The duality of my personal reality in which I lived and had struggled to accept now was understandable.

I spent many nights with some of the senior guides and even more listening to the masters. I heard them speak the truths and philosophies that I had inherently known and followed but had forgotten during my life on Earth.

They spoke of the continuation of life, and how what we call death is just a new (and different) life. They explained that death and birth really are just transitions, a shifting of awareness. When you die, your awareness goes from a restricted viewpoint to a wider, more expansive viewpoint. As your physical body slips away, you return to a form that is closer to what and who you really are. This slipping away from the physical world enables your perspective to widen to its true insightfulness.

> **From the masters:** "You are as dead now and alive now, as you ever will be. Existence does not rely on the physical body. The physical body is no more than a "tool" which you use to experience the human/physical condition. You are who you are—and we do not mean that you are your physical self. No, rather you are much more than that.

"You create for yourselves a world, a reality, and then you populate that reality with forms you call bodies and people; but those forms are you, and those realities yours. So, when you decide you have had enough of that form and that reality, do you allow the form to cease existence—or in your terms, die. The form, which is energy from you, is reintegrated with you to be re-used in another reality as another form; so, all is continuous and everlasting. Nothing is ever lost nor is anything ever extraneous. All is.

"Because you (the souls participating in the physical world) perceive yourselves as only the body or the form that you observe, then when that form ceases to function, do you presume that you, too, cease to function. But this is not true. Only the physical form that you were using while in the physical plane is ceasing to exist. You, the real you, goes on forever. For you are part of us all, and we are part of you, and we exist always.

"The fear of death is merely the fear of the unknown—or rather, the forgotten, because it is not so much unknown, as it is forgotten. It is only through the incarnation process that you have caused yourselves to forget. You create forgetfulness to more easily enjoy, join with, and participate in the various "plays" or scenarios you

create for self once on the physical plane.
Therefore, the concept of dying fills you with fear,
for you suppose there is either some judgment or
a vast nothing and both terrify you.

"However, there is not one who would judge,
there is only you. You have chosen your life and
you have chosen your death, so only you can
decide whether to call the life "successful." But to
us, all lives are successful; for all lives create
experiences and all experiences add to the whole,
which is all of us.

"Essence does not die, only physical matter dies;
and that is only a discontinuation of essence's use
of a particular body. However, essence will
manifest another body with different
circumstances and a different personality to
continue the lessons on the earth/physical plane.

"This does not mean we do not understand
sorrow; nor does it mean that you should not be
sorrowful. It means you should also rejoice, for
life truly is eternal. There is not an end to life, but
rather, just more experiences gained in a
different form."

I spent as much time as possible with the masters. I
was learning (or should I say, relearning) information
that would help me not only live my own life in a

more holistic way, but it would also help me as I resumed my job as escort.

One of their discourses was about those returning to a physical existence. They explained that when you are (re)born into a physical form, your awareness becomes restricted. This is because you now need to focus your awareness and attention through the physical body you have selected. You need to forget about everything else and just focus on the reality in front of you.

> **From the masters:** "Each soul is, unto itself, a separate and unique individual with unique and separate goals, desires, and lives. The focus of each soul is pinpointed toward the reality in which the body dwells, and it is that which the soul sees as real. No longer is it part of the expansiveness; no longer is it part of everything...now it just the individual who dwells within the physical world."

Some souls find that making the shift between the expansive focus of being part of everything to being just a separate individual isn't always easy. In fact, it can sometimes be a bit traumatic to find your focus so limited. So, as escorts and guides we not only help those leaving the physical world, but we also remain within calling distance to newborns to help them make this transition. We give them reassurance when they need it, and offer guidance and advice, when requested.

Remembering the Astral Plane

PEOPLE CALL THE astral plane Heaven, Paradise, Elysium Fields, the afterworld, the great beyond, the eternal rest, the great unknown, the happy hunting ground, the hereafter, Hell, Purgatory, Hades, Limbo, Perdition, Another World, a different plane of existence, and a thousand other things. Me, I just call it *Home*.

It's the one place I feel comfortable, accepted, and when I return from there, I'm always happy—silly, blissfully, awesomely happy.

In simple terms, the astral plane is a layer of reality just outside of our awareness. It shares the same space as our reality, but it can only be reached when you're in spiritual form. physical bodies don't exist in this realm; they aren't needed.

That doesn't mean there isn't a type of matter; there is. Astral matter exists, but unlike physical matter it's much more pliant and responds to thoughts and emotions so easily that it can seem like magic.

Primarily, light, music (sound), and emotion comprise life in the astral plane. Emotions are extremely focused, and they play an integral part in the lessons and tasks that are part of the astral plane. And there are tasks and jobs and lessons to learn just as in the physical plane.

The astral plane is a place, and yet it's also an experience. It's a different type of existence than what most of us expect, and it can sometimes take getting used to.

Many of us come to the astral plane with certain expectations. We may expect to experience choirs of angels or golden gates leading to peaceful meadows filled with meditating monks. These (and more) are all possible and will remain as long as we need or want them to. But trust me, after a few decades, you'll get tired of the peace and quiet (most souls do), and you'll be ready to move on to something more meaningful. And the astral plane can be that for you, too.

The astral plane is a type of school room. In some ways, it's an extension of the school room we call Earth, and in other ways it's even more extensive than that.

If your goal is to return to the physical plane for another life, then the astral plane is an extension of the Earth school room. If, however, you wish to move on to other things, then it becomes more of a high school and junior college. (I consider the plane beyond the astral plane more of a university, while the plane beyond that is your graduate school.)

There are, at least as far as I know, seven planes of existence.

The physical and astral planes are the first ones encountered by most people. After all, we live in the physical plane, and we often visit the astral plane during dreams or when between lives.

Each of the seven planes gives you the tools and freedom to learn, explore, and gain more insight and awareness. Each one helps you bring more vision into your life (physical and spiritual), and each one helps you understand what life is about.

The seven planes are kind of like a giant loop. You start out at the Tao, moving through the other planes based on what you want to experience and learn, and eventually you work your way back to the Tao.

While I know of the existence of these other planes, I only know a little about each of them (primarily from "lectures" given by the masters that I've attended on the astral plane).

My awareness (and limited expertise) is about the physical and the astral planes.

Overlapping Realities

For the most part, what happens on the astral plane stays on the astral plane; however, there are some things that can (and sometimes do) affect our own world.

When these overlaps in reality occur, people can sometimes think they're encountering ghosts or some other supernatural or paranormal beings.

But while ghosts make wonderful topics for books, movies, talk radio, or reality TV shows, the truth is that spirits stalking the living, trying to interfere with our lives, repeating their last dying moments, or wandering freely unaware that they're dead are extremely rare.

Ghosts and Hauntings

From the masters: "As we have stated, the concept of a ghost does not truly exist. What does exist is essence not incarnate (astral-constrained souls) attempting to contact or communicate with those participating in the dramas of physical life. This is usually due to a soul's refusal to let go of the life just ended. They are so immersed in the physical realm and the dramas there, they fail to accept the fact that they are no longer incarnate."

SO, WHILE IT'S fun to scare ourselves and get that adrenaline rushing with the thoughts of possibly encountering some headless horseman doomed to ride through the town every Hallow's Eve, the odds of any of us encountering a haunt, haint, ghost, or spirit dwelling in the physical world is next to nil.

Most often what we physical beings take for ghosts is one of the following:

- Echoes from emotionally charged objects or areas

- Souls that stay in proximity to loved ones to experience their own funeral (however, they are almost always accompanied by a guide)

- Manifestations of vaporous images, objects moving, or odd noises (which are usually created by the person encountering these images or occurrences)

- Souls remaining in the physical world because they don't know they're dead, seeking revenge, seeking justice, seeking to help, warn, or comfort the living, because they are overly attached to someone or something (this is extremely rare)

Most people have this belief that ghosts are souls hanging around the physical world because they either don't know they're dead or because they refuse to leave. However, while this can occur, it is rare. Mostly, it's our own fears leaking through. We're afraid that we'll be stuck in some sort of limbo, neither here nor there when we die, and so we label that fear *ghost*.

This fear is then bolstered by occurrences of paranormal phenomena that people attribute to ghosts. For instance, many youngsters with psychic abilities tend to lose control of their abilities while going through puberty. Books or magazines may tumble from shelves, odd noises may occur (such as bangings on walls or footsteps in hallways or on stairs), and cold spots can appear in otherwise normally warm houses. While most people attribute this to hauntings and ghosts, it is merely the havoc created as a result of the youngster's burgeoning powers coupled with their newly raging hormones. Once their body settles down, the powers settle down and settle in.

Other times, a soul may opt to have the full death experience, which includes observing his or her own funeral. Sometimes they need to see and experience that to recognize the reality of their own deaths. Family or friends who are intuitive or even slightly sensitive may pick up on the energies of these visiting souls (because souls who remain almost always are accompanied by at least one guide). But while they may be ghosts in a technical sense, they rarely linger and they're not seeking justice, revenge, or anything else. They simply want to have the full death experience.

For a soul to remain in the physical world, the soul needs to imbue so much of his or her own energy into some part of the life that they actually create a cord to it (similar to the chains that Marley the ghost forged for himself in the book *The Christmas Carol*). It's these heavy energy links or cords that can help the soul remain in the physical world even after the physical body is dead.

However, most people don't do that, and unfinished business is not a strong enough tie to keep you linked to the physical plane. Especially when you have escorts, guides, and counselors to help you understand and realize that life goes on, and whatever was unfinished or hurtful in one life can be addressed in another life at a different time.

Music is Key

THE PHYSICAL BODY holds a major part in helping us maintain the frequency of our reality. Each plane of existence (Physical, Astral, Causal, Mental, Buddhic, Messianic, Tao) vibrates (exists) within a set range of frequencies. In musical terms, each plane is a specific grouping of notes. If, for instance, our physical world contains the notes middle C, C#, D, D#, and E, then the astral plane would start at E#, which is right next to E.

So, in our world each person's physical body acts as a balancing tone, keeping them centered within the appropriate range of frequencies, within the appropriate musical chord.

However, when you die, your frequency shifts because the body is no longer there to center it. This is when you should be on the threshold between the physical world and the astral worlds. But if you created auric cords between yourself and your business, your family, or some other part of your life, you've created a tether tying yourself to the physical world.

This tether can become a partial replacement to the physical body in as much as it helps your soul retain the frequency needed to maintain a physical plane focus. But it is a poor substitute since it can never fully replace the physical body.

Instead, you aren't physical, and you can't (fully) interact with the physical world. But then again, you probably wouldn't care. Most people who create these types of cords don't.

If you corded a person, you can, by drawing on that person's energies, remain in the physical world. However, it will eventually kill the person you're linked to, and then you will both lose your connection to the physical world you were trying so hard to keep.

Creating and using this type of link with someone will cause an imbalance between you (a karmic debt). You may think you're staying because you love someone so much that you can't bear to let go, or you may believe that they can't possibly function without your help, or some other (to you) valid reason, but all you're doing is creating an imbalance between you.

Now, there are a rare few who end up with these types of links through their altruistic endeavors. They have dedicated themselves to some cause, issue, or their family to the extent that the link was forged, but once they die, they are ready to move on, and so the link becomes an *unwanted* anchor. Escorts and guides can help them get free and move on.

Sometimes you might create cords thinking that you can continue to influence how a company is run, or who it is sold to, or how the church functions, and if you are able to draw enough energy from the connection, you might have some influence.

However, if you maintain the link for long, you will eventually create negative energy areas. These are dead areas; areas where living people feel uncomfortable. For instance, there may be a building, a park, or a street corner that people unconsciously avoid.

People may get the shivers, feel on edge, get angry, or suddenly feel unhappy when they visit these dead areas. That's because the negative energy retains the emotions which people then unconsciously experience. The experience makes people so uncomfortable that they simply avoid that spot whenever possible.

It is this type of negative residue, these echoes, which end up as stories of ghosts haunting the building or the park.

What are Echoes?

Echoes of the past are quite common and are caused by extreme emotions. How many times have you walked into a room and known that someone has had a fight? There may be no one except yourself in the room at that moment, but you know that within the past day or even the past hour, several people had been arguing in there.

Or, perhaps you walk into a room and you can feel

how much the people of the house love each other. Again, no one else is around; you're not observing anyone, it's just the echoes of the emotions that they've left behind.

Those types of echoes usually only last a day or two. However, if some couple owned and lived in a house for 30 or 40 years and fought every day, then the echoes of that anger might last a decade. The same is true if the couple showered each other with love and respect for 30 or 40 years; again, the echo of that would last a decade or so.

Emotional echoes like this would most likely be felt by others as either negative or positive responses to the house.

Some historic sites carry powerful emotional echoes. American Civil War battlefields can be very negatively charged areas filled with anger, fear, and the cries of the dead, dying, and wounded. The same is true of many of England's and Ireland's castles and battlefields. Most areas where people were tortured, imprisoned, or brutalized for years or decades, will retain the negative echoes for centuries (multiple victims over multiple decades leave huge negative echoes).

Battlefields, places of terrorism, scenes of torture or mass murder, these all retain an imprint of the emotional scenes experienced by the victims. The more emotion expended, the more likely that someone will feel that it's haunted.

The emotions discharged at the time of the event seep into the buildings and grounds nearby. The more the emotions occur, the more deeply it becomes imprinted on the area. Now, for most people who come along later, what they'll feel or sense is a chill (negative emotional echoes) or a warmth (positive emotional echoes). Others might feel the left-over emotions—fear, lust, hate, anger, agony—and while they don't really see anything, the sensations are enough to have them believing in ghosts.

There are others who are even more intuitive, more sensitive to the nuances of the energies around them. These folks can really see the events—maybe completely, maybe only partially, or maybe just in short snippets—but it's enough to convince some people that they're observing ghosts. However, what they're really observing is the recording of the event caused by the emotional energies.

Now, let's throw in some of the physical manifestations that can occur. Most often, these are caused by the living, not the dead. Usually the living person or people want to see a ghost or a ghostly manifestation so much that when they experience the emotionally charged surroundings, they create the physical manifestation.

Focused thought does affect matter; there are hundreds of accepted, published, and documented studies from universities such as Princeton, Duke, and even Edinburgh that show this. Yet, most people are so desperate to believe in ghosts that they don't even consider that they themselves might have caused the ghostly event. But when you have a group of people all focusing on the same idea, matter does move; things do shift; and suddenly you have a ghostly appearance of a vague, white, amorphous shape.

While souls in the astral plane can manifest in the physical world, few have a need or desire to. That's because once in the astral plane, souls are busy. Life (after death) is not all idleness.

The 7 Levels of the Astral Plane

THERE ARE SEVEN levels to the astral plane.

- Transition
- Rest
- Review
- Learning
- Decision
- Awareness
- Integration

Each level has a different purpose, and not every level is accessed by every soul between lives. It all depends on what the soul needs or wants to accomplish while in the astral plane.

For those who are long-term residents of the astral plane or working in the astral plane, all levels are available. However, for those moving through the astral plane either on their way back to the physical plane or onward to the causal plane (the next plane beyond the astral), you usually need to complete each level in succession.

If, for instance, you're moving from the physical world to the astral world, you would need to do the tasks associated with the Transition, Rest, Review, and Learning levels before moving on to the Decisions level. The last two levels (Awareness and Integration) are completed when you want to move onto the next plane (the causal plane).

There are no borders or barriers indicating where one level starts and another one ends. The levels are more internal than external. The distinction between levels has more to do with the types of tasks and experiences each level offers.

You could think of each level as a separate country, and once you learn the customs and language of the country you're in, you move on to the next country, and the next, and so on. (This is a metaphor, not a literal example.) In look and feel, all levels are equal; however, in terms of tasks and experiences, each level is quite different.

The Transition Level

THE MOST COMMONLY viewed and visited level of the astral plane is the transition level. That's because it's where people transition from the physical world to the non-physical world, or vice versa, which puts it closest to the physical plane.

Some people (like me) deliberately move between the physical plane and the astral plane, but most visitors are accidental tourists. These accidental tourists include dreamers, people having drug-induced out-of-body experiences, or people who are transcending a traumatic experience (moving out of their body to avoid extreme pain or emotion, or during a near-death experience).

Others who aren't so accidental include people meeting with their guides/angels/guardians or deceased loved ones. What they all have in common is that they all end up in the transition level of the astral plane. Of course, you'd have a tough time believing that after listening to each of them describe their experience. That's because the transition level is rarely the same for any two people.

If you were to ask me to describe the transition level,

I'd say it looks like any other Midwestern town, large city, palm-tree-filled jungle, Greek fishing village, South Sea island, mountain top, or farm. In other words, it looks any way you want it to. In its natural state, it's sort of a vague, gray, nothing. I usually see it as a fog-filled gray void, a blank canvas just waiting for my brush.

Focused thought or extreme emotions, or rather the energies behind them, are what create the reality. It works pretty much the same way in the physical world, but it takes much less energy to form the reality in the astral plane. This is primarily because the energy of the astral plane is less obdurate and more pliable. In fact, the energies of the transition level are so easy to manipulate that actions and thoughts can appear magical.

The minute you think of something, it's there. You want to be in New York? The energies shift so quickly that it seems you just appeared in New York. (Actually, the energies literally create a version of New York around you.) If you want to be at your childhood home…you're there. Like I said, magical.

Unlike the physical world, though, there is no cohesive, universal agreement as to how the reality will look in the astral plane. Therefore, the topography changes to suit each person.

However, if there are several people together with differing thoughts and emotions, then the reality changes to fit the most focused or the most emotional thoughts. For instance, if two people are in the transition level together and one is expecting a seashore and the other a large city, and they have equally focused images of their expectations, then they will each see what they want and expect to see. But, if one of them is ambivalent about their expectations, then that person will most likely see their companion's reality.

Emotions play a large part in how the reality of the transition level (in fact, the whole of the astral plane) looks and feels. Because the energies of the transition level are so pliable, they react quickly and easily to your emotions. You could be happy and content standing on a sandy beach with waves and the sound of sea gulls, when you remember something that makes you angry. Suddenly, sand is stinging your face and body, while the water surges toward you and grabs at your feet as it tries to drag you out to sea. Your calm beach day just became a raging hurricane.

Of course, if something like that happens, you simply need to damp down your emotions and refocus your energies. It sounds difficult; but end up in enough hurricanes or volcanoes and you soon learn (or remember) how to curb those wayward emotions.

I say remember, because we've all been there (in the astral plane), probably hundreds of times. It's just that most people forget going there or visiting there. Or if they do remember visiting there, it's clouded in a dream-like memory…vague, ephemeral, and not quite real.

In fact, one of the jobs of escorts and guides is to help you remember. We also work to keep the reality balanced while you're remembering. We nullify (as best we can) your emotional output so that your reality meets your expectations without any sudden shifts to hurricanes, earthquakes, or volcanoes.

I remember an incident that really helped bring this point home to me. It was during one of my early solo sessions. My guide had stepped out of the picture (so to speak) so that I could try controlling things on my own. I had created a peaceful English garden, complete with birds and trilling fountain. I was debating about adding a cat to lounge in the pool of sunshine on the stoop of the cottage, when suddenly, there was a young girl of about twelve standing on the steps.

In a flash, the sunny peace of my garden was gone. Instead, we were surrounded by one of the worst thunderstorms I've ever seen.

Rain fell in torrents. It was nearly impossible to see anything. The rain was so heavy, I needed wiper blades for my face. Lightning flashes streaked the sky, and they seemed to be growing angrier and angrier with each flash.

Suddenly, shingles flew everywhere as one of the bolts of raging electricity struck the roof of my cute little cottage. I shrank back, my fear and anger surging forward at the wanton destruction of my construct.

I blinked to clear my vision. Opening my eyes, I regarded my visitor. The girl's face was scrunched up and her hands were fisted at her sides. I stormed two steps forward and stopped as the wind gusted forward with me. I was only adding to the melee of the storm with my anger.

Taking deep breaths while focusing on the colors green and blue, I let my energies drop in a slow, easy calm. Pushing those calming energies outward, the raging storm quieted to a simple Spring rain. Adding even more quieting thoughts to it, it soon became a summer sprinkle, and then even that became just a gentle mist.

I went over to the girl and she opened her eyes as I approached. They were filled with the pain of loss and the fear of being alone. Gripping her in a hug, her hands unfurled. As her sorrow turned to sobs, she wrapped her arms around me as if to ensure I wouldn't leave. She clung to me like a kitten whose claws become entangled in your clothes.

When her crying quieted, the mist and gray clouds began to dissipate. Stroking her hair, I asked, "Why are you here? You don't belong here."

She wasn't part of the astral plane, her presence was too translucent, so I knew she still had a presence in the physical world. However, she also didn't appear to be your typical accidental tourist.

She pulled back far enough to look up at me. Then she swiped her hand across her tear-streaked face, as she answered, "I miss my mom."

We sat on the steps, weak sun beams shining down and the cat I had been debating about adding to my scene was now conjured and sitting in her lap.

Stroking the cat and letting its purrs soothe her, she finally divulged her story. After her mother had died in a car accident she had been devastated. So devastated that she had refused to accept her mother's death and clung to her emotionally.

Her desperate need had created such a tight bond to her mother that one night during the child's dreams, that need had brought them both here. Having worked the once, the little girl then made it a nightly habit to focus on her mother as she was falling asleep.

The girl's intense connections to her mother had enabled the little girl to cross over and meet up with her mom for almost a year. She admitted, though, that recently it had been getting harder and harder to do.

Communing with my sources (which means checking with members of my crew through our linked energies and auras), I found that her mother hadn't been here (in the transition level) for several months. Instead, one of the many guides had been trying to wean the girl away from the need to make the memories of her mother real.

Tonight, when this girl had shown up, the guide had been busy with someone else. Frustrated and overwrought, the girl had created a literal and emotional storm that had overwhelmed my test.

"I know you miss your mom, but she's not here anymore. She's moved on. By coming here all you're doing is recreating your memories of her," I ran my hand down her hair as she began to weep again.

"While that isn't a terrible thing, it isn't helping you. You need to let go and move on." Lifting her chin, I made her meet my eyes. We talked about her needs versus the needs of the soul, and whether it was right for her to keep her mother from moving on with her life. We also spoke about how unhealthy it was for her to keep clinging to her mother.

One of the key lessons that escorts and guides learn (and then try to pass on) is that while it's okay to mourn (in fact, it's healthy and necessary), it's not okay to cling.

Mourning is for Everyone

Mourning is a valuable coping mechanism for everyone—the living and the deceased. However, some people get stuck in their grief and are unable to move through it. When either the living or dead cling, they end up creating cords between themselves and the other soul. These cords make it difficult (if not impossible, at times) for everyone to move on.

If the deceased person continues to cling to his or her old life, they not only keep themselves from moving on, but they can affect those left behind in the physical world. The cord of emotional energy can affect the moods and thoughts of those they cling to.

Also, if the living refuse to release the deceased, refuse to complete their mourning and move on, they can create a net of emotional energy so strong that the departed soul can't move on. The soul becomes stuck in the lower levels of the astral plane heeding every call and prayer uttered by those they left behind. They are forced to remain in a limbo-type existence— neither living nor allowed to move completely into their spiritual existence.

This emotional stagnation is unhealthy for both groups, and counselors (both living and spiritual) will do their best to help eliminate these types of bindings.

Many times, it is these types of relationships that mediums focus in on. Finding an honest and competent medium can sometimes be as beneficial as counseling or psychotherapy. This is because many times what the living need are reassurances and closure, something that honest mediums can usually give them.

This is also true of those in spirit form. Many times, what they need is also to be reassured and convinced that they can (and should) no longer mingle with and interact with those in physical form. They need to move away from the physical world, which they are no longer a part of, and begin the tasks necessary to become part of the community of souls that inhabit the astral plane.

While it may seem cruel, letting go is the kindest action of all. It allows everyone to move forward with their lives (physical or spiritual), and it helps everyone grow spiritually.

Of course, letting go doesn't mean forgetting. Remembering is one of the best ways of letting go. By remembering our loved ones—living or dead—we find that they can always be with us, without anyone creating unhealthy tethers.

Time will erase the memory of a face, but it doesn't erase who we've become because of having known (and cared for) a loved one, a cherished friend, or special relative. And those who have died also carry with them every memory, every recollection, and every emotional hug that they received or shared with you.

One of my experiences as an escort brought that point home in a very poignant way. She had died one night, quietly in her sleep, so we met in the living room of her house. Although she realized that she was dead, she was reluctant to leave.

She remained in her living room gazing around at all the things there. Then she reached up and pointed to a photo of her daughter and grandchildren in a handmade frame. Several times she tried to grasp that framed photo, but each time her hands only went through the photo. Finally, she wrapped her arms around herself, and slowly turned to face me.

Then she pointed at the photo, and then at me. Regrettably, I shook my head. I couldn't grab the photo for her any more than she could grasp it herself.

If souls could cry, she would have. Even so, her despair was palpable. Reluctantly, she kissed her fingertips, and then "touched" them to the photo. As she continued to stare at the photo, I told her, "All you can take with you now is your memories and your love," and I touched her heart.

She nodded sadly, understanding, but not totally happy, and we crossed over.

So, while we all find it difficult to let go, we must. Even the masters spoke about mourning and its necessity to help all of us cope.

> **From the masters:** "For those remaining as humans within the physical plane and who now must cope with the loss of one who was friend, lover, brother, sister, or other, we say this:
>
> "Rejoice for them, for they are not gone. Rather do they remain with you forever. Weep for yourselves, for you have lost one whose place in your lives cannot be refilled, and whose absence will be sorely missed."

"We do understand, and we know that the loss and missing of one can be painful and difficult. Mourning is a normal and appropriate reaction. How one mourns is up to each individual, for each must find their own means of coping. It is easy to explain that the person, in essence, is not gone, but the person in flesh is the one with whom you laughed, talked, shared, and interacted with. It is this interaction that you will and do miss, and for that there is no miracle to relieve the absence or the pain that the absence causes.

"But again, does it become each one's experience, not just for a day, but for the entire event. How they deal with the event is their experience and will be shared by all, even that one whose absence they are mourning.

"We see the absence of some as agreements made for those who will remain, for they would learn or experience the numerous ways of coping with that loss. We see some absences as being of the accidental kind. In these instances, do both those remaining and that one absent go through a period of mourning, because that one having left not of their choice, also needs to adjust.

"So, there are many reasons for departure and many reasons to remain—for everyone—but only each soul should decide when, what, where, why, and how (to stay or go).

"If one would ease the transitioning for both themselves and those who have died, would they do well to address their anger, hurt, or sorrow, to that one whose absence they do mourn. This allows both mourner and fragment (who has) left, to clear the air and heal as the energies are exchanged and the emotions are realized by both.

"By retaining the emotions, turning them inward, or by directing them toward others or objects other than that person who has died, do you deny both self and the one [who has] gone that healing, that release. In feeling your pain (and the departed do feel it) do they experience the grief and anger or relief and joy caused by their departure.

"Through this shared experience can those departed then choose how to reply, for they can respond, and most will do so. They can respond with loving, caring, calming; or with hatred and anger, or they can respond not at all.

"Communications and emotions do not end because the (physical) form has stopped functioning. If anything, those who have left human form, need that emotional contact to continue, for many are unsure, hesitant, and afraid. Granted the anger most mourners feel is

132

grievous to those no longer within body, but it is also understood to be a type of caring, for one would not be angry if they did not care.

"These emotional links aid both [souls] during the transition of death and can aid both [souls] in moving on with their choices. So, do not dismiss the one who has died from your life and your mind, but instead include them in your thoughts, in your mind, and (if you wish) in your dialogues and conversations.

"Some believe themselves foolish or crazy to continue speaking with loved ones who have died, but we tell you that the information is not lost in some void. Rather do the emotional links keep the communications open and aid all involved in moving ahead.

When those who have died wish to discontinue with that communication, will they ease the linkings between you until all are balanced and able to move on. This is true of those remaining within the physical, also. For they, too, will begin to ease the links, when they feel the grief lessen. The need for the linking will thus lessen and they will feel more at ease and ready to move on.

"Is it crazy to speak to spirits? We do not believe so, for all do benefit from the conversations."

The Stages of Mourning

Each of us needs to mourn and move on. Of course, mourning isn't something that everyone does the same way or in the same span of time.

According to psychologists and grief experts, there are seven stages or phases to mourning:

- Shock
- Denial
- Anger
- Bargaining
- Guilt
- Depression
- Acceptance

Each phase can take one day or several months to complete; it depends on the person and the situation.

People who have been ill or who were caring for someone who was ill, may or may not experience shock, just as others may seemingly go straight to acceptance, only to sink into depression later. Many of those I've escorted go from shock straight to denial and anger. Others have jumped over shock, to denial, and then straight to bargaining.

However, guilt or depression is usually the phase where people (both physical and spiritual) get stuck, and it is during these phases when guides or counselors are the most useful.

When a returning soul gets stuck in the guilt or depression phase of mourning, we do our best to counsel them and keep them from remaining fixated on loved ones back on Earth.

One way we do that is to move them out of the transition level of the astral plane, so they can no longer easily view or watch those on Earth. However, this becomes difficult if those on Earth have also become stuck in the guilt or depression phase of their mourning, as this is when those tethers get created.

If both those on Earth and those in the astral have become fixated in one phase of mourning or another, then the emotional pull and turmoil created between them becomes almost too much for either of them to bear. The souls of all those caught in the web of emotional energy become drained and those around them begin to be affected.

Emotional trauma is very real in the astral plane, and it can be very destructive. Therefore, we (the escorts, guides, and counselors) work hard to keep these types of emotional entanglements from occurring.

However, sometimes the tethers are too strong, and the emotions too deep, so the soul who just returned will opt to be reborn as quickly as possible. There is little to be done about this; it is their choice, after all. But if a soul opts to return to Earth without completing their mourning period or life review a lot of residual and not-understood emotions are usually brought along.

This can (and does) create major complications for them in their new life. They may have crippling feelings of guilt, but because they no longer remember why, there's no way for them to alleviate it. That's why it's always better if the soul can take the time to work through their previous life and make some plans about their new one before just jumping right in.

From the masters: "Emotions can easily be carried from life to life if left unresolved. The difficulties arise when the cause, person, or object of the emotion is not known or recognized by personality and may not exist in the current lifetime. This causes the emotion(s) to become overwhelming and consuming.

"When the person cannot determine who or what the anger is directed at, it becomes directed at all—all people, things, events, places, just everything. This then overwhelms and colors the entire life and may cause innumerable other reactions.

"If not resolved between lives or before the end of the life in which the emotion was generated, these types of emotions can literally alter all plans made for the next life.

"If you have agreements to marry but cannot resolve the anger and hatred, the agreements may all be abdicated simply because either you or they cannot cope with the adverse emotionalism. This, then, would be an instance wherein a teacher or friend who could do so, would be helpful in aiding the person to understand the unresolved negative emotions and put them aside until they are truly needed, which may be some other life."

The Rest and Review Levels

THE NEXT TWO levels are rest and review. Their
purpose is exactly what their names imply. If a
returning soul had a traumatic life or a highly active
life, the next step is rest, otherwise, they go onto
review.

Examples of a traumatic life might include a life
where the person was born, and then starved to death
by the age of three; or maybe, they were held prisoner
and tortured for years before dying; or they might have
been killed unexpectedly, perhaps when a bomb
exploded, a plane crashed, or when a building burned.
All these instances would probably cause a soul to
want to drift for a while to allow themselves time to
recover.

Another type of tumultuous life might include one
where many deaths occurred due to the actions of a
single person. And if the person responsible for all
those deaths had also died, that person would need
time to recuperate. The person responsible would need
to work through all the guilt, anger, or hatred that had
caused them to act the way they did.

Rest and recuperation are needed by many souls at

various times of their development. That's because
energy does not like to remain in an agitated state—at
least not soul energy. So, after a life of trauma and
turmoil, souls want and need to rest emotionally,
mentally, and spiritually. This allows your energies to
calm so that you can focus on the next steps of your
spiritual evolution.

Reviewing what was learned in your physical life is
the next step. The review of a life just completed can
be done in many ways. The most common method is
through contemplation and meditation. However, you
can also incorporate re-enactments or recreations into
your review.

This can be done by creating a movie-like recreation
of events and situations from your life. These
projections can then be viewed by you and any others
you want to include. For instance, if you prefer a
counselor or guide to help you understand what the
lessons were in a particular life, event, or situation,
then recreating a projection of the event is quite
helpful.

However, you can also recreate the experience using
astral matter, and then having other souls, guides, or
escorts stand in for the other players in the drama.

Some situations or life events may require more
interaction than a simple review of your memory of
the event. Perhaps, you need to immerse yourself
within the drama again, or perhaps you need to
experience it from a perspective other than the one you

had when you lived it. To do that, you can recreate a situation much like you would in a drama class.

Perhaps in life your spouse cheated on you. When you recreate this drama, you might take the part of your spouse to better understand their reasons, motivations, and emotions. You might even take the part of an observer as a means of understanding the overall situation from the perspective of an outsider.

Using Constructs

If your drama has all the major players, but you need other people (like bit players) to populate your scene, you can also create *constructs*.

Constructs, or projections, are built of astral matter and are formed based on your thoughts and emotions. They can be extremely detailed or just vague shapes. It all depends on you.

If you have strong feelings about the construct, then you will most likely create something with more detail. However, if the construct is merely window-dressing for your re-enactment (such as someone to fill in during a crowd scene), then the construct might appear more vague, less detailed.

Of course, if you don't remember how to create a construct, then a guide or escort can help. Although it doesn't really matter whether someone participating in your drama with you is an actual soul or a construct, there is a way to tell the difference. Constructs don't glow, or at least not the way a soul does.

This is because souls are part light and part music. Although, astral matter is too, its structure is more akin to inanimate matter in the physical world. Therefore, constructs simply don't shine the same way a real soul does.

One of the most common constructs that people want, expect, and need (and one that I'm very adept at creating) is a personification of death. Death has appeared as dark and sinister, young and roguish, mysterious, creepy, male, female, human, and monster.

If someone fears death and thinks it will approach like some spectre in a black cowl and robe carrying a scythe, then that's the death they'll meet. After all, what you see and experience in the transition level is what you expect and what you create (sometimes with a little help).

The Purpose of Reviews

But whether you use constructs or have real people participating in your drama, the whole point is for you to have a chance to review what happened so that you can learn from it.

You can select which aspects of the life just completed you want to review, or a guide or counselor can work with you to help you determine what portions of your life to review. The purpose of reviewing any part of your just-completed or any other physical life that you lived is to help you understand where you might have done things differently, why other participants in your life reacted the way they did, and to help you understand what the overall purpose or lesson of that event was.

Many of our life events are to help us understand concepts such as acceptance, compassion, generosity, or love, but often we become so lost in the emotional drama that we miss the more subtle message behind the event. By going through the review cycle, we can step back from the emotional impact, if we need to, and see the more subtle issues.

The review sessions are to help us become more aware and understand why we made the choices in life that we did. We can choose to review every event, every detail of our life, or we can select just a few. It's entirely up to each of us and what we want to learn and understand.

Not everyone waits until they're dead to do a full life review, or to review just a particular event in their lives. Sometimes people take excursions to the astral plane to go over some aspect of their life that is troubling them.

This is because learning is easier in the astral plane since the astral plane focuses and heightens emotions. This heightening of emotions makes the re-enacted scenarios much more intense and memorable.

The astral plane counselors and guides can be helpful and are always willing to assist, which also draws many people to the astral plane when they are experiencing extremely troubling or tumultuous times in their physical plane lives.

Understanding How the Past Affects You

My current specialty is (for now, anyway) life reviews, and it's a skill that sometimes gets carried over into my everyday life here in the physical world.

I had just been introduced to a young man and when I shook his hand a montage of his past lives flashed into my mind. It was like seeing several movies all fast-forwarding as the images and information uploaded into me. It wasn't every life he'd ever lived; it was just those few that were impacting his current life.

I saw him as a young man, a fisherman. He was happy with his life. His time out on the boat catching fish and working with his brothers and friends brought him a lot of joy. I then saw their fishing vessel caught up in a powerful storm. The boat floundered and began to sink.

He and three others managed to escape on the skiff. However, none of them had grabbed food or water before casting themselves adrift in the small boat. They also had no oars, and no way to make a sail, so they drifted at the mercy of the sea. They floated under the cruel hot sun for several days, and he began to regret some of his choices in life before he finally succumbed to dehydration.

I then saw him taking part in a battle. He was wearing leather armor and carrying an axe. He was fighting for a cause he didn't believe in and for a man he didn't respect; however, he had had to join the army or his parents would have lost the small farm they leased. Because he preferred growing things to killing things, he didn't last long. A member of the opposing army gutted him with a pike, and he died slowly and in agony as the summer sun beat down upon him.

Another life and death that flashed past me was of him and several friends. They carried bows and rifles, but the rifles were not of a modern type. All of them were barely into their twenties and had been lifelong friends from the same nearby village.

They were in the woods hunting and one of the guns went off accidentally. He was shot in the abdomen (in the same area as when the enemy soldier had stabbed him with the pike). The pain was crippling, and he begged his friends to help him. But instead of seeking help for him, his friends abandoned him in the woods to die.

Just as I saw these pasts, I also knew that this man had sun allergies and a gastrointestinal problem caused by the unreconciled emotions created during these past lives and deaths that I had just seen. He and I became friends, and through that friendship, I learned that my knowledge regarding his health issues was correct.

We spent time talking about reincarnation and life in general, and I was able to help him resolve his fear of the sun, ocean, and forests, and he was also able to come to terms with his feelings of anger and regret that these pasts had created in him.

He had commented how often he would feel such anger or regret but had no explicit reason for these feelings and having nowhere or no one to direct them at, he continued to bottle them up until they resulted in stomach and eating issues. Now, having a better understanding of why he felt as he did, he was able to move forward with his life while leaving these unwanted emotions behind.

> **From the masters:** "Any lessons or experiences not fully inculcated (during the life or during the review period on the astral plane) will be held over within the root chakra. It can then reappear within the next life as flashes of memory unexplained by any current life experiences. Also, can it reappear within the current life as allergies, fears unexplained and not understood, or undiagnosable aches and illnesses.
>
> "Fear turned inward like that becomes a toxin to the body. Therefore, is it best to spend time on the transitional level inculcating lessons, working through experiences, and discharging any extraneous emotions, because those, too, can carry over from lifetime to lifetime.

"For instance, if you have a fight with someone (an intensely emotional argument) that ends not to your satisfaction, and you then die—perhaps of a heart attack—and if you do not work through that anger in the astral plane, you can then return (to the physical world) with that anger still in you.

"This anger, having no point of direction, no focus, can then color the entire life. This can lead to aborted tasks, agreements, and monads as others find themselves unable to cope with the overwhelming, unfocused anger. It may even cause irreparable harm to the body because as the anger seeks an outlet, a point of focus, it begins to tear at the body and aura of the one who is angry. This tearing can appear as ulcerations of the digestive system if the anger is swallowed, or as heart problems if left as an unchecked emotion."

In another instance, I met a young lady during a business gathering. She found me a good listener, and so spent the dinner break telling me of the issues she was having with a married couple she and her husband were friends with.

Evidently, she and her husband liked the couple a lot, and they had spent many an evening at the couple's home. However, every time it was her and her husband's turn to reciprocate, she found herself unable to issue the invitation.

Each time she imagined this couple inside her home, something inside her just froze up. She said whenever she even thought about the couple being in her house now, she was physically ill, (headaches, fevers, nausea).

She told me that the other couple had never shown her or her husband any reason to doubt the friendship, nor did she have any doubts about the honesty of the couple, yet she couldn't bring herself to have them at her house.

I hesitated to speak up, but after thinking it through, decided the worst that could happen is that she concluded I was a nut. (I've had that reaction from people before, and I've survived.) So, I proceeded to explain to her what I had glimpsed when we had shaken hands.

She had known the couple in a previous life, only at that time the wife was an old man and the husband was the old man's granddaughter.

The town where the old man and his granddaughter had lived had been overrun by hostile invaders, so they had fled with the few provisions they could scrape together.

It was the middle of winter, and they had little in the way of warm clothing. They had travelled through the countryside, camping out in the frozen woods, with no shelter and little food. When the granddaughter had become ill, the old man had risked everything to seek out help at one of the farmhouses near where he and his granddaughter were camped.

The young lady I was speaking to at the dinner function was the person who responded to their knocking. A young girl of about twelve at the time, she was frightened and refused to allow them inside despite the old man's explanations and pleadings. Her parents and her younger brother were already ill with fever and she had all she could do to take care of them.

The old man implored her, and she threatened to sic the dog on them. Eventually, he crept back down the stairs, and he and his granddaughter hid in the barn. The temperatures plummeted, and a blizzard enveloped everything. Two days later, she found the old man and his granddaughter frozen to death in the barn.

She was horrified, and never forgave herself. It became an imbalance, a debt, which she felt she owed them. She believed that if she had allowed them inside the house, they might have survived.

She carried that weight with her all through that life, and into this one where she now had a chance to balance things out again. Her reluctance to issue an invitation for them to come into her house was her fear creating barriers. Those fears were also turning inward, where the guilt was making her experience the same types of physical reactions that she imagined the old man and his granddaughter had gone through in the barn.

Once she realized that the couple held no grudges from that previous encounter (they wouldn't be friends with her and her husband if they did), she was then able to forgive herself. That not only helped her remove the barriers, but it also helped her to stop making herself sick over it.

Once she issued the invitation to the couple, she said it felt like everything suddenly just fell into place. By issuing the invitation, she brought everything back into balance.

I don't get flashes from everyone I meet, and I can't always help everyone I get flashes about—mainly because not all of them are willing to listen to me or allow me enough access to their lives to help them.

Sometimes people are merely passing through my life, and all I can do is acknowledge (to myself) that they have unresolved issues, and then hope that they give someone else a chance to help them deal with the issues.

The Instructional/Learning Level

THIS LEVEL IS the most classroom-like of the entire astral plane. There are instructors and masters here who will discuss assorted topics and issues. You can meet with them one-on-one, or as part of a group.

The masters are integrated souls (blended souls— multiple souls melded together) whose knowledge includes all physical reality (and not just Earth), the entire astral plane, and a lot of what is waiting for us on the causal plane. (Many of them spend time on the lower causal levels just as some of us in the physical spend more and more time on the astral. They share their knowledge of the causal just as we share our knowledge of the astral.)

In sharing their knowledge, they are helping themselves learn, and it is through that sharing and learning that they can then move on to the next phase of their lives.

They understand how the physical life experience works; they understand about physical life lessons and goals, and they understand about the subtleties of human and soul nature. As integrated souls, they have the memories, experiences, and knowledge of each individual soul. This helps them see a more global picture and better understand the nuances of human interactions.

For instance, a master may have up to 10,000 souls blended into one, and perhaps all those souls experienced at least one life as a mother to at least one child. They can, by merging all those memories and experiences of being a mother, understand how our choices as a mother or as a child affect our lives— long- and short-term. And they have a better understanding of the many choices that a mother and child can encounter and make.

The masters have a better understanding of the dramas that we all create for ourselves. This enables them to offer insightful and valuable advice as to what it all means, why we participate in these lives, and how we might learn from our own chosen lessons more easily. The masters are the ultimate astral teachers having both patience and insight, along with a great willingness to share with anyone who wants to learn.

The instructional/learning level is also the place where you can experiment. You can try out different scenarios in preparation for your next physical life.

Perhaps you want to see what having certain personality traits would be like. This is the place where you can try them on and see. You can establish a set of circumstances, put on some personality traits and see whether it might be something you want to try in physical life. Maybe you want to find out what physical reality would be like based on a specific socio-political configuration.

It's also here that someone (like me) might practice astral matter manipulation and hone their skills at nullifying emotional outbursts.

There are any number of skills and insights to be learned on this level.

There are areas here for learning about what types of jobs exist on the astral plane. There are even counselors to help you figure out just what job your skills are best suited for.

It's at this level that you may want to intern for a specific career, or you may choose one or more opportunities to shadow someone to learn about their job to see if it interests you.

There are countless opportunities to learn about the different career options, observe souls as they work, and even (in some cases) try out some of the different jobs to determine whether you might want to take them on.

This aspect of the instructional/learning level isn't just for those who are done incarnating, either. You can (as I have done) explore these types of ideas between lives. Then once you decide on something, you can begin training (again as I am doing), so that once you have decided to remain discarnate, you're already on your way to a career.

I don't want anyone to think that the souls in the astral plane are running around in suits and ties in busy cityscapes. It isn't like that. Life in the astral plane is not geared toward rewards of money, advancement, power, or objects. The whole point of the astral plane is to learn more about relationships and emotions, to strengthen your ties with your fellow souls (whether incarnate or discarnate), and to learn about helping, loving, caring, and acceptance.

Jobs and tasks are taken because you want to do them, not because you must. The rewards are the spiritual and emotional growth that you gain. You can spend years, decades, or eons in the instructional/learning level just studying, experimenting, and trying out different jobs or taking on various tasks, or you can take up a hobby and spend your time painting with emotional colors, creating music using the tonalities of energy, or sculpting astral plane matter. It's your choice.

Rules are more internal rather than boss-enforced. Those who dwell on the astral plane already know and understand that anything they do (negative or positive) has consequences greater than themselves. Therefore, if you agree to take on the job of guide, you understand fully what that means.

Perhaps, you decide you just don't feel like showing up for work one day, and you also don't feel like notifying anyone that you're not showing up. You must then endure the consequences of that choice.

In the astral plane, those consequences are more direct than here in the physical world. In the physical world, if you duck work and don't tell anyone you can get scolded or maybe even fired. However, when you don't show up to help the souls transitioning between physical life and the afterlife, you will suffer their confusion, fear, and angst. You will be inundated with their anguish and their need…that's part of the agreement you make when you take on the job.

If you had notified one of the other guides or escorts of your desire to take a break, then the responsibility (and consequences) for those souls would have shifted to them. So, as I said, it's a learning experience for everyone involved.

We're all interconnected, and the astral plane is a key tool to reinforcing that memory for each of us. Every time we act, negatively or positively (in fear or in love), the consequences of our actions are direct and nearly immediate. So, we don't need someone to warn us against playing hooky, we have our own methods of knowing what loving behavior is and what it is not.

The Decision Level

THIS LEVEL GIVES you the tools and assistance you need to make decisions about your future. It is one of the most important levels for everyone. It's here that you can make major choices, small choices, global choices, and very personal choices. The counselors and advisors work closely with those who come here. They also work closely with the instructors on the learning level to help souls make the best choices they can for themselves.

The primary choice that most souls need to make is whether to incarnate, remain in the astral plane, or move on to the causal plane. Of course, once you make that choice, there are many more choices to make. As part of the decision level there are many guidance counselors available to give you advice and help you understand all the potential opportunities that are offered.

Deciding What to Do

Many souls move between the decision level and the instructional level numerous times as they try out things while deciding what they want to do. They may come to the decision level thinking that they know what they want, but as they start to make their choices, they realize that they either haven't thought through everything, or they don't know enough about some part of what they were choosing to make an informed decision. Therefore, they go back to the instructional/learning level to find out more or try something out.

It's not uncommon for a soul to make one or two decisions, and then return to the instructional level, and then come back to the decision level and make a few more decisions, and then repeat the process of returning to the previous level.

Very few souls realize just how intertwined our choices are. We may think it's simply a matter of choosing to be reborn in in Europe in the 1600s CE or in the Americas in 3200 CE, but there's a lot more to it. This is because each choice you make spawns more choices while it also eliminates others. It's a continuous process of choices building upon choices, until the basic structure of the chosen life is perceived and acceptable.

Of course, not everyone is that picky. Some may just take whatever comes along, not caring about the ramifications, but simply allowing everything to happen by chance. Neither way is right or wrong, and both ways will gain you experiences, and that is, after all, what life (both physical and non-physical) is all about.

Going

If you decide to reincarnate, you might start by deciding what your goals and purpose will be in the next life. You may want to experience deprivation, war, or unrequited love, or you may go the other way and experience riches, stardom, or power. You may want to see life from the perspective of someone who has mental or emotional issues, or you may want to see the life through the eyes of someone who's race or ethnicity is rejected by society.

Multiple Player Scenarios

Many life experiences (or lessons) start out as a type of framework. You can select the framework of teacher/student, betrayed/betrayer, mother/child, siblings, abandoned/abandoner, supporter/supportee, or any of the millions more that are available.

How you fulfill these experiences…well, that's up to you and those participating with you. It's all about the choices you make. You may select to be part of the mother/child scenario as the mother. However, you may choose to spend most of your time pursuing men, a career, or whatever pleasures suit your fancy instead of caring for your child. You may decide to watch TV, drink, use drugs, or do almost anything rather than pay attention to your child. Those are all choices you make once the scenario begins and you are incarnate.

But maybe you've already done the scenario from the aspect of the mother, so in this lifetime you choose to be the child. You now need to work out things with the other participants from last time, since the person who was your child last time should take the open role of mother. This is because it allows you both to see both sides of the mother/child lesson.

If you partner with someone to complete one of these multi-person scenarios, then you should continue incarnating together until you complete the experience. This is because these are shared experiences. So, to achieve a balanced perspective, you both need to share the experience throughout the multiple lifetimes it takes to reach that balance.

Single Player Scenarios

Of course, not all life lessons require multiple players. Some lessons are self-contained. Perhaps you want to see what it's like to be in a society where those of a certain body shape, skin color, or accent can limit or expand your choices and experiences. These are all self-contained lessons.

By giving yourself selected attributes, you can then experience life from a certain perspective and make choices based on that perspective. It may be that you are extremely talented but because of some prejudice expressed by the people around you, you are unable to fully explore that talent. You might choose to fight against the prejudice, give up your dream of using your talent, commit suicide, or some other option. Whatever choices you make, will contribute to your overall life experience.

Timing is Everything

Another choice that should be made is the time frame in which you will be born. Because time has little meaning in the astral plane, you can choose any reality in time you want. You may choose to be born into a reality like our 16th century France, or you might prefer something more Star Trek-like. Future, past, it's all there...you just need to decide.

Making Choices

You can also make smaller choices, such as whether you wish to be male or female, your personality traits, your ethnicity, what major milestones you want to try to accomplish, and what major stumbling blocks should occur in your life.

All the choices you make feed into each other. You can choose every aspect of your new life, or none, or maybe just a few aspects. It's up to you. Of course, there are no guarantees that anything you plan will occur. This is because all those involved in your life (you, your parents, siblings, friends, etc.) make choices. Sometimes their choices complement yours and sometimes their choices abrogate yours. Of course, all this leads to even more choices until the life ends up nothing at all like you planned it. But that's the fun of it. After all, it's all about the experiences.

If you're not sure about some of the choices you're thinking of making, you can go back to the instructional/education level and create mock scenarios to help you visualize what might occur based on your choices.

For instance, if you're considering reincarnating in a reality where perhaps World War II never occurred, you might want to create a mock world to see what types of socio-economic-political situations this type of reality might have and how those situations might affect your choices of gender and ethnicity. Will it help you achieve the goals and experiences that you want, or will the combination become a major stumbling block?

Another major consideration when choosing the who (you will be), what (you will do or learn), where (you will be), and when (you will appear) is whether you have any outstanding imbalances to fix.

Choosing to Fix the Imbalances

Imbalances (also known as karma) can occur when choices you make override or abrogate someone else's, or when choices someone else made overrode or abrogated yours. The most commonly understood one is murder.

If you murder someone, you have just removed all their choices; this creates a major imbalance between you and the person you murdered. Most times, this can be fixed by you experiencing the circumstances from your murder victim's point of view. However, if both participants have gained enough enlightenment, occasionally other means of regaining balance can be found.

Sometimes the balancing of karma can be very emotional and drama-filled. Because of this, it can take most of a lifetime to balance one instance of karma. Other times it can simply take a couple of astral meetings to work things out.

The amount of difficulty is driven by the age of the souls involved, and by their acceptance or reluctance to put things right.

In this lifetime, I had an instance of rebalance that I thought would be difficult, but it ended up being rather easy to accomplish. That was because we both wanted to correct things between us.

The imbalance was incurred during a life as a Japanese businessperson. I was fiercely competitive, as was my main rival. But the strangest part was that we enjoyed the competition. We both thrived on it, and so did our relationship. We developed a camaraderie based on our rivalry with one another and we relished the ability to shock the other with our daring. Every day we strove to find ways to steal the other's best customers or to find another (better) way of marketing our goods.

However, as the years progressed, the competition somehow got the best of us, especially when the economy began to dip. I found a way to manipulate my competitor into making a bad deal, and in shame, he killed himself.

That left the company vulnerable, and I bought it, paying less than it was worth. But what I learned that day was that although I had made a great deal on a company, I had no one to share it with; I had no one to gloat with. It wasn't the competition I had loved so much, but the friend I'd had to share it with.

In this life, I met my rival when I joined the company where he worked. We were friendly, enjoyed working on projects together, and even enjoyed the same type of humor and similar pastimes (books, music, and movies). However, there was a certain lack of trust between us that we both felt but couldn't seem to overcome.

To get it resolved, we both went out at lunch time and did a meditation by the nearby lake. Meeting on the astral plane, we recognized the issues immediately. Our past was getting in the way of our present, and because of what I had done then, we were both having trouble creating the trust that we wanted.

We met astrally several more times, and each time we grew in our awareness of each other. This awareness helped us recognize the spiritual growth we had both made. While I had hurt him then, I was no longer that person, just as he was no longer my competitor and the man I had shamed with my manipulations.

We were both more than those people now; we had grown and changed, and in that changing we had learned. We had learned that while competition can be fun, friendship was better. Winning his company from his family hadn't been fun because he had no longer been there. The fun had come from the rivalry we shared.

It might seem an odd type of relationship to most people, but still it was a friendship. Winning wasn't the point of it; sharing the triumphs and the defeats with each other had been the point.

Once we recognized and acknowledged the truth of all of that, we found we could trust one another again. Now we had an even stronger friendship than when we had been rivals in Japan.

We had both learned that friendship was the key, not competition, not winning, not things. No object in this world would ever be worth as much as the friendship we rediscovered and rebuilt. It's a concept that each of us should always remember, in every life we live— without friendship, no one wins.

But whether an eye for an eye is needed, or something less final or destructive is acceptable, you still need to consider whether your new life is conducive to correcting some of those imbalances you may have collected.

Of course, you can always leave everything to chance, and just dive right into a new life with no forethought or consideration; the options are yours.

Staying

Staying in the astral plane is a valid option. And staying presents you with a myriad of choices. There are artistic pursuits, learning and educational opportunities, and, of course, the proverbial rest and relaxation option (just to name the high-level choices available).

Completing Your Lessons

If you have physical life lessons that were left incomplete, you will most likely have to return to the physical plane (eventually), but the choice of when is up to you (and whomever you need to interact with to complete the lesson, unless the lesson was a self-contained lesson).

If the lesson (or experience) involves more than just yourself, then you need to consider everyone else's wishes and schedules. If the person you need to complete the mother/child scenario with is anxious to get that lesson completed, then you might have to forego staying and take on another life first.

If the others involved in the experience are willing to wait, though, then you can take a break from corporeal existence to attend school or take a vacation. Then when the other participants are ready to complete the lesson with you, you can return to the physical plane together.

Moving On

Moving on to the final two levels of the astral plane is a joint venture. While you can decide that you've learned all you want from the physical plane and so choose to stay in the astral, moving on requires the agreement of your crew.

Each soul starts out with a group (or crew) of other souls that they spend most of their time with. This is usually around 1000 to 1500 other souls (although this is not set in stone and can be less or more).

Not every member of a group is required to incarnate, so there is almost always some of them who are full-time residents of the astral plane while they wait for those of their group who are spending time in the physical world. However, once most of the group decides to move on, the rest begin to finish up their physical lives so they can join the group in the astral plane.

In physical plane terms, this can take hundreds of years. After all, all the incomplete life lessons need to be completed, and any imbalances created in the physical plane need to be taken care of. So, moving on is not a quick decision. It's a decision that takes time and patience, as everyone in your group gathers back together.

While the whole group, or crew, needs to decide to move on (to the next plane), the individual souls can move on to the awareness level once the choice to move beyond the astral plane is made. This means that while a hundred members of the crew are still participating in lives on the physical plane, another thousand or so can be gaining experience on the awareness level.

However, the whole crew of souls should progress through the awareness and integration levels before they move on to the causal plane.

The Awareness and Integration Levels

I KNOW LITTLE about these two levels, primarily because I've never had much call to spend time there. These levels are for those moving on to the causal plane. The souls who migrate to this level are souls who have spent time on the astral plane and have learned all they wanted to there.

Obviously, I'm not one of those, because I'm still corporeal with a lot left to learn about the astral plane. While this doesn't keep me from going to the awareness level, it does give me little reason to spend a lot of time there.

Awareness Level

I do know what happens on each of these levels, though.

The awareness level is for gaining greater awareness. It enables you to gain a wider perspective, which will help you transcend the astral plane and move on to the next plane of existence.

There are representatives from the causal plane there

to help you understand and broaden your perspective. These representatives are called masters, and they share their wisdom and understanding with those who wish to learn.

I have spent some time listening to them while on the astral plane, and I've spent time in the awareness level during meditative sessions. What I have learned from the masters is amazing. (I've shared some of their insights in this book. However, there was so much more from them that I wanted to share, so I wrote the companion book, *Choices*.)

Integration Level

The integration level is where groups of individual souls merge into one entity. Although merged, they can still share their memories and knowledge instantly because they still retain bits of their individuality, as well as their individual memories.

They are not Borg-like nor do they have a hive-like mentality. They are as loving and caring as a Mother Theresa would be. They may not be as human as…well, as a human is, but they are certainly not alien or inhuman, either. They simply seem to have a better understanding of what it means to be human, while also having a wider perspective as to the human condition and what causes it.

Perhaps once I spend more time on the astral plane, I will be able to better explain what integration is and how it's done. If so, I'll see what I can do to make the information known, since I probably will no longer have a physical form to write with. (But maybe I can play muse to some budding author in the physical world.)

Three Transitioning Guidelines

I WAS PREPARING to tag along with one of the guides as part of my job refresher sessions, when the guide popped in and asked if I remembered the three transitioning guidelines. (These are the three standard rules that each escort and guide follows when helping someone transition between planes.)

Feeling somewhat proud of myself for remembering them, I recited them smartly:

1. Each soul selects his or her death (and birth) experience.

2. Escorts and guides do not interfere with your experience.

3. No one dies (or is born) alone.

These are extremely important to remember, for us and for you.

Rule 1: Selecting the Death (and Birth) Experience.

WHILE YOU MAY not understand this (or even believe it), deaths (and births) are unique experiences that can only be experienced in the physical plane. Therefore, each person seeks their own experience for entering and leaving the physical world.

For instance, you may have gotten the flu, and while it can be nasty, it can also (most times) be cured. However, while sick, your soul may decide that this is the perfect vehicle to use to exit the life. Your life lessons are completed, your life's goals are accomplished, and so your soul decides to move on.

Note: Some lives are interrupted when other people's choices override their own (terrorist attacks, some plane, train, or car accidents) or when nature erupts and catches them off guard (earthquakes, floods, hurricanes/typhoons, or other types of disasters). But even during these types of deaths, the soul can make choices, which we abide by.

> **From the masters:** "Death, like birth, is a very individual experience because it is one created by

self for self. No others create the reality, only you.
If one were to die with a blank mind, then one
would most likely experience nothingness when
they transition. However, we see most people
relying on those beliefs, those stories, told/taught
them when they were children.

"This is because the stories are simple and easily
visualized. Few would find themselves guilty of
sins grievous enough to preclude their
advancement to heaven; therefore, do they,
within those final moments, seek that which
brings them the greatest comfort.

"Essence is not afraid, but ego is, and ego does
not become discarded as easily as does the
physical form. Ego is needed if one is to go
through the review phase of the astral plane. It is
not required that you do this, but many choose
to. So, until the choice can be made as to whether
the review will be done, the ego remains with
essence.

"This is why so many people experience some
sort of death or afterlife, such as heaven, hell, the
meeting of loved ones, or other, because it is
ego's fears and needs that require these images
and essence (the soul) merely experiences it."

So, what does that mean for us, the escorts and guides? It means that no matter how much we may want to change things, no matter how upset we are by the circumstances of someone's death, no matter how much we might want to alleviate their pain and panic, it's not for us to interfere. We shouldn't (and don't) change things. Which is actually rule number 2.

Rule 2: No Interference

NO MATTER HOW difficult a person's death might be for us to witness (because we feel their pain and fear—physical, mental, and emotional—just as they do), we will abide by their choices. For instance, if the person we've come to help cross over seeks to endure the pain and degradation of being dragged through town, and then stoned to death, we will abide by that choice. If, however, the person seeks the emotionalism of that death, but without the physical pain, then we will abide by that, too, and so will help them rise above the physical pain.

The adage of "I feel your pain" isn't just words for escorts and guides. We do feel the pain of those we're trying to help. However, we can moderate the connection between us and those we are helping, so we're not overwhelmed by their pain or fear. Knowing the pain and fear, on all levels, though, is how we learn and understand. It's one of the reasons for taking on this job. It keeps us human and it keeps us compassionate. But it isn't the only reason.

I can sense more than a few of you squirming and wondering why anyone would choose this. Why experience the fear and pain of death repeatedly?

Because we also get to experience the joy, exhilaration, hope, and wonder when they realize where they are.

We are there when each soul realizes that their life isn't over. We are there when the pain stops, and we are there when the wonderment and awe appear. That's our reward…to experience the joy and ecstasy with each person who has crossed over and now realizes that they are still alive.

It's not a feeling you can easily express in words. The exhilaration of seeing someone realize that they are alive in spirit form is akin to the joy you might experience when you witness the birth of a child. Yet, it's more than that.

Of course, not every soul feels joy when they cross over. Some souls are so vested in their physical life that they refuse to acknowledge the death of their body or that the physical life is over. They cling to the vestiges of that life, refusing to release their hold on a something they are no longer a part of.

One of my first transitions was such a person.

The Book Shop

She wouldn't leave the book shop. She wouldn't listen to anything I had to say. The book shop had been her life, and no amount of coaxing from me was going to make her leave it.

She had been 42, married and the mother of one. Her husband was at home with their son while she had been busy working at her bookstore. It had been her life, more so than anything else. Unfortunately, she had had an aneurysm and died almost instantly. In fact, it was so sudden and unexpected that she hadn't yet registered that she no longer had a physical presence.

When I arrived, she was agitated and upset, and she began berating me for not helping.

"We need to call the police," she turned to me, her hands on her hips. " I need this gone," she waved an arm at the body face down on the floor behind the counter.

I nodded, glancing between her and her body that lay on the floor behind her. The body was face down, so I sort of understood why she wasn't recognizing herself. But even so, the clothing, the hair color and style, and even the shape of the body should have been giving her some idea of who the person was. Yet, she still could not, would not, comprehend that it was her.

She flung a dismissive hand at me, "See what you can do. I'm going to call the authorities."

She turned away, pulling a cell phone from her pocket. Deciding to let the scenario play out a bit further, I stepped toward the body.

Her face turned stormy as she spun to face me. She

thrust the phone back into her pocket and growled, "Figures. I can't get a signal."

"Well," she turned her anger toward me. "What do we do? Did you give her mouth-to-mouth? Is she going to be all right?"

Noticing that the body was still face down, she muttered, "Typical. I always have to do everything myself."

She squatted next to the body and tried to turn the woman over. Instead, her hands went through the corpse.

After several tries, she turned to me. I watched the realization of the situation slip across her as piece by piece her face fell into a mask of disbelief.

She stumbled to her feet and backed away from me and her body.

"Who are you?" She buried herself into a corner and continued pushing as if hoping she could push herself right through the wall.

"Just a friend." And I was. I wore a copy of the same body I wear in life, and I was dressed in jeans and a top; nothing scary. No black robes, no scythe.

I smiled and held out my hand, "We need to go now."

She squirmed against the wall again. Then her eyes

squinted, her eyebrows drew together, and she squared her shoulders. Standing straight, she gave me a wicked little smile, and shook her head. "No. I'm not leaving."

It was as if she had finally realized that I wasn't some monster, and I didn't want to force her to go with me. I was simply here because she had originally wanted an escort when she died. However, she seemed to have changed her mind.

I tapped into her energy to see what her concerns and expectations were. What I saw was that while she hoped her husband and son wouldn't be too upset with her for dying, she cared too much about her bookstore and what might happen to it if she left. So, she had decided she wasn't going to leave.

She was afraid that if she left with me, her husband would get rid of her dream. She loved that bookstore. She had sacrificed a lot to buy it, build it up, and keep it going. In her mind, her family had never appreciated it, nor had they appreciated how hard she had worked to make it so profitable. She had struggled against the big, generic bookstores that had come to town, and she had won. She had beat out most of the competitors in her small town, but above all, she just loved that bookstore.

She saw her son and husband as being all about sports, NASCAR, and hunting, while she was all about books and reading.

I knew that nothing I told her was going to convince

her to go with me. However, I did try coaxing her with the promise that she could always live another life focused on books. However, she was too preoccupied with the life that had just ended and her beloved bookstore to care about future possibilities.

Yet, I wouldn't (couldn't) just leave her here. It was this type of behavior and close-mindedness that caused stories of hauntings to start. Her attachment was so deep that she was unable to let go. She so wanted someone to care about that shop as much as she had, as much as she still did. And, while that connection remained strong, I knew it was going to be difficult to get her leave.

Because she wouldn't leave with me, I had to call in a guide. A guide could stay with her indefinitely to help her through this situation, while I (being corporeal) would eventually have to return to my own physical body.

The key was for this woman to acknowledge that she was dead so she could move on. However, it appeared that she needed to go through the whole scenario of the body being found, identified, examined, and buried.

If I had left her there to wander without focus or assistance, she would have prolonged not only her own agony, but also that of her family.

I was told that once she figured out and accepted (more or less) that she had died, she opted to return to the physical plane almost immediately. She evidently had no patience for working through any of her lessons or issues from that life, nor did she care to do much planning for the next one.

She was one of those souls that is very tied to the physical world and what it offers, and so that's where she wanted to be.

Of course, not every soul is that fixated on the physical world, but it does demonstrate one of the reasons for rule number 3.

Rule 3: You're Not Alone

From the masters: "Always are you not alone, for there are souls who would aid, support, guide, and comfort you when transitioning between worlds."

EVEN IF YOU choose to die alone, at least one escort or guide will be present; we simply make sure that our presence is not detected. This allows us to fulfill guidelines 1 and 2, while still ensuring that a soul isn't left wandering or wondering what has happened.

One of my first experiences with fulfilling this guideline for someone was difficult (for me, and I believe for my charge, too). But it was what he wanted.

I arrived in a dark alley, and it took me several moments to locate the person I was there to escort. I finally spotted the young man's broken and battered body tossed amidst some refuse near an overflowing dumpster.

Someone had beaten him severely and he was dying. The physical, emotional, and mental pain were nearly overwhelming, and I pulled my connections to him back a bit to dim the experience for me. Still, I felt the anguish, confusion, and anger emanating from him in intense waves.

I knew from his aura that he wanted this experience of being alone and in pain. It was part of a bigger whole. Dying this way and feeling this pain (both emotional and physical) would help him carry these emotions over into the next life.

This experience would color the interactions he would have, not only with those who had hurt him in this life, but also with other people who might act in a similar or resonating manner in his next life. This was about more than just dying; this was about learning how to forgive your enemy; learning how to feel compassion even when you've been badly hurt (physically or emotionally).

If I had made my presence known, it would have alleviated some, if not most, of his anguish, anger, and loneliness, but that would have ruined his whole plan. Therefore, I remained out of sight until his body was no longer capable of supporting life, and then I escorted him across.

For him, the transition was instantaneous. There was no lingering above the body; no white light; no heavenly chorus. He went from life to death while remaining in the darkened alley with the broken body. That is what he wanted. I merely recreated his reality in the transition level of the astral plane and in a blink of an eye relocated his soul to the new reality.

This memory would be stored on his soul's aura as part of an incomplete lesson (as all such memories are stored). It would then be pulled forward into whatever life he was living at a time his soul deemed the lesson applicable.

For instance, in the next life, he might find himself in a situation where he loses his temper and is about to respond in anger using his fists or some other blunt instrument. However, the situation would pull forth feelings of déjà vu and compassion because of these stored memories. He would then have the choice of overriding this memory and letting his anger loose or allowing this memory to help him overcome his impulse to inflict pain, and so grow (spiritually). All of that because he retained the memory of his own beating death in this life.

> **From the masters:** "Emotions can easily be carried from life to life if left unresolved and if they are strong and intrinsic to the death. If you are feeling anger and hatred for someone and are hit by a car and die, then that anger and hatred stays with you. There is no resolution from the previous life. This can be a lesson to be carried over to another life or a problem to be resolved."

Seeing and Reading Auras

From the masters: "Those aiding souls in transition try to acclimate those souls to their new surroundings. Since we (all of us in essence) have no true physical form, escorts and guides are often perceived by the one transitioning as someone they expected to see—grandmother, brother, husband, or others—and the surroundings are those that the one transitioning also expected.

"Therefore, if the one transitioning expected heaven then that is what they see, if they expect St. Peter, then that is who will greet them. If they expect nothingness, then that is also provided."

SO, HOW DO I know what you're expecting? How can I know if you want to die alone or with company? I have become (as have all escorts and guides) very adept at reading auras and emotional energies. (It's not mind reading...thoughts are always private unless you want to share them. The connections are there to share them, but so is the respect for and understanding of privacy.) But whether in physical or spiritual form, you have an aura and auras contain a lot of information.

Being able to see auras is another of those oddities that I've learned to do. Of course, being back on the job, so to speak, I now understood why I needed this particular talent. Before, it was just one more thing that set me apart from most other people.

Even for those who aren't death escorts, auras can be interesting and informative. I couldn't always see them. It was a talent I discovered after my skating accident.

Head Banger

We lived near a swampy pond that was the "Walt Disney World" of fun and entertainment when I was growing up. In the spring, there were tadpoles to catch, and caterpillars to watch. In the summer, there were frogs, lightning bugs, and dragon flies, plus (once the water and mud dried up) hillocks and gullies to ride our bikes over and through. Come the fall, there were reeds and mud wallows; and in the winter, there was ice skating.

The thin skim of water would freeze over, and we'd hack down the reeds to leave a stubble of lumpy ice. On that stumpy ice pond, we'd hold hockey matches and skating races.

I was probably one of the world's worst skaters. Combine that with the stubbly nature of the pond, and

I was an accident waiting to happen.

While trying to stay out of the way of the older kids, who were playing hockey, I tripped over one of the bumpy patches of ice and landed hard on my back. My head smacked into the ice, leaving me out cold for a couple of minutes. When I came to, I had a headache the size of Texas. Not feeling well, I headed for home.

Even then, I was noticing a strange rainbow of colors around people and things, but I just thought it was because of the smack I took to my head. However, when the colors were still there the next day, I became a bit worried.

I told my mother about the fall and the colors, and she hustled me off to see the doctor. He said it was a mild concussion and I would be fine in a couple of days. The headaches went away, but the colors never did. However, I didn't tell anyone about still seeing the colors because I didn't want anyone to drill a hole in my head.

When I had told my girlfriend about the colors, she was quick to let me know how someone her parents knew had been seeing things that weren't there, and they had drilled a hole in his head to fix it. I certainly didn't want that to happen to me. So, as far as anyone was concerned, I was fine. There were no rainbows around people.

It was years later when I found some books in the library that explained about the energy fields that surrounded people. The books stated that everyone had an aura and that these emanations were part of the electro-magnetic field generated by our bodies.

The explanations and images included in the books were enough to help me understand that what I was seeing wasn't completely aberrational. The colors surrounding people were evidently real; but I couldn't find much material to explain why I could see them and others couldn't.

Again, it took another few years to discover that the aura isn't generated by our bodies—or at least not just by our bodies. Rather, it's the energy generated by our body, mind, emotions, and soul. While a great many theories have evolved as to why some people see auras and others don't, there's never been any definitive answers (that I know of). All I know is that after smacking my head on the ice, I could see what others normally couldn't.

Over the years, I have encountered a few others like me…that is, people who can see (or at least sense) the auras around people. We've compared notes and, while we don't always agree 100% on what the meaning is of each color or shape in a person's aura, we do agree on most of the information.

Again, I tend to think that our disagreements are due more to a difference in interpretation than anything. Because what each intuitive sees or senses is still reliant on how they define and interpret the input. And what filters (of personality) they see the world through.

What do Auras Look Like?

The first thing I notice when I look at someone's aura
is the intensity and the shape. Believe it or not auras
come in many shapes and sizes, and it rarely mimics a
person's physical shape and size.

However, a person's physical shape and size can
influence the shape and size of an aura. For instance,
many children's auras are rather spiky and the colors
very intense. This is primarily because there is a lot of
energy trying to fit into such small packages.

Obviously, all children are not the same, so not every
child has a large, spiky aura. Kids who are older (in
terms of soul age) usually have quieter auras—the
older the soul, the quieter the aura (usually...but it's
not a hundred percent correlation). Of course, since
there are more high-school-aged souls than any others
on Earth, most of the children I encounter have fairly
noisy auras.

Also, the health of the physical body does play a part
in the intensity and the shape of an aura. So, if a child
is ill or malnourished, then obviously the aura will be
less intense, more collapsed, and usually without the
spikiness of a more robust, normal child.

In adults, the shape and size of auras is varied and can
be greatly influenced by mood or health, but other
things can affect the aura, too.

Shape and Size

As I said, one of the first things I usually take note of when I observe someone's aura is the shape and size. Auras that are sharp and spiky (in an adult), pulled tight (like a very tight spiral), are too close to the body (within six to eight inches of the body), are spinning in a counter-clockwise direction, or any combination of those, usually indicate some sort of negativity.

Auras that are rounded, soft, flowing clockwise, expansive, or any combination of those, usually indicate positivity.

Auras that appear scattered, meaning that they either contain flares of colors bursting at odd moments, or have stringers shooting off and away from them (originating at the mental center), indicate a lot of mental activity that is either not very well focused or is not coherent (some mental patients have these types of auras, but then so do some highly creative people).

Of course, if the flares or stringers are bursting from the motion/action center, it means that someone needs or wants to move; that the inactivity is causing a build-up of energy that needs to be released through some type of movement. You can often see this in athletes or in people who tend to act first and think about the consequences later, especially if they are stuck in a situation where their movements are limited. Many of these types of people can find a release through pacing, tantric breathing, or jiggling their leg or foot (if they're sitting).

Colors

Colors also play a large part in the information that you can obtain from auras and chakras. Based on the chakra you look at, colors mean different things.

Some of the information you can glean from observing the colors of the different chakras or the different layers of an aura are:

- The emotional attitude at the moment of observation

- The mental attitude at the moment of observation

- The physical health (if observed while on the physical plane)

- The chakras' and aura's health (whether any of the chakras are blocked, too narrow or too open)

- The past or future lives that might be impacting the current life

- The connections (familial, sexual, emotional, or spiritual)

- The karmic ties

- The soul's age, role, and personality filters chosen for the life

That's a lot of information. It's little wonder then that many of us who can see auras have learned to put up blocks. Imagine standing in a room with ten other people and being inundated with all that information from each of them. Talk about information overload. Forget about trying to live your own life, you'd be too busy trying to sort out all the information you're getting bombarded with.

Blocking the Noise

I PARKED THE car and stood for several moments in the dimly lit parking lot. I took a deep breath relishing the quiet breeze and the sparkling stars that illuminated the sky. I turned my gaze from the dark pond to the low, utilitarian building behind me. My shoulders slumping, I trudged toward the entrance of the building as I tried to prepare myself for another grueling 12 to 14 hours of hell.

The moment I stepped inside the assault began. Voices yelled across the vast warehouse-like space as people tried to be heard above the beeping and whirring of the hundreds of fax machines, jangling phones, and buzzing intercoms. The cacophony reverberated inside the giant metal box and set my teeth on edge.

I wove through the maze of long, folding tables (the type usually used for banquets and conferences) trying desperately to close myself off to the other "noise" that bombarded my senses—the "noise" of unwanted emotions and thoughts.

Unable to escape this prison, I had to cope with the mass of emotional energy that clung to everything and attacked me the moment I stepped inside. The one-two punch nearly made my legs buckle, and I was glad that I hadn't eaten anything before returning to work. Of course, there hadn't really been time; I had left work at midnight and after a two-hour drive had arrived at home. A brief two-hour nap and here I was, back again.

They called it a "war room" and for me it was a war— a war filled with emotional onslaughts that nearly crippled me each day I came in here.

Personally, I didn't understand why I couldn't do my job at my real desk—a desk surrounded by quiet—but they wanted everyone even remotely connected with the project here in the war room, ostensibly so we could all feel the camaraderie. Rah! All I felt was nausea.

I swung my briefcase onto the table tucked into a corner as far from the melee as I could get. I had claimed this corner from day one, and most people were happy enough to leave me alone in my little corner.

Four hours later and desperately needing a break, I nearly ran from the building to escape into the brilliant spring sunshine. I stood amazed for a moment, just enjoying the quiet that fell on me like a cape once I stepped outside.

I walked over to the pond and sprawled on the grass. Just as I began to feel some of the tension trickle out of my shoulders, I heard a voice sail across the parking lot to me, "Hey, we need you back here. They're crashing the program again."

I sighed audibly, reluctant to leave my quiet sunshine. However, I dragged myself to my feet and headed back feeling like a condemned prisoner heading to his death.

As I looked at the building, I could see just how ugly the aura around it was—all red and spiky. Emotions were high, everyone was tense, on edge, and the energies now pulsed around the building like an angry boil. I shuddered and closed my eyes not wanting to see what I was walking into.

Just before crossing the barrier into that oozing barrier of nastiness, I pushed my few reserves of energy forward as a barrier against the energy of the war room. Then I grabbed the door handle and stepped inside.

When I had first been temporarily moved to the war room, my shields had been strong and secure. As the days extended into weeks, my shields had thinned, and my energies had dwindled. I no longer had much left, and every day was a struggle to keep my sanity in this morass of negativity.

When I reached my corner, I saw Tim (otherwise known as *the Irisher*) had arrived. He was now situated at the table nearest mine.

I enjoyed his company for several reasons, not the least of which was his strong aura. When he was around, his aura, which was rather expansive to begin with, usually covered mine, lending me an additional block against the "noise" of the war room. Of course, I also enjoyed his Irish wit and charm, along with that wonderful accent of his. So, seeing him, always improved the day.

I was just getting back into the swing of my own work when *she* came over. She was one of the most abrasive, opinionated, I'm-always-right people I had ever met, and for some unknown reason she had decided that we were best buddies.

She toddled over to my table, pulled out a chair and began yammering at me. She told me of her latest infatuation, asked my advice on how to snare this new possible beau—I said I'd think on it, having no intentions of helping her in this regard—and then she told me about the latest escapades of her dogs (she had five).

All of sudden, I heard, "WILL YOU SHUT UP AND GO AWAY!!!!"

She and I both whipped around to stare at Tim, who was still working away counting forms and setting up stacks of forms for faxing. I started to turn toward the others in the room, when I caught a small quirk at the corner of Tim's mouth. I looked at him more closely, but he again seemed busy with his forms.

No one else in the room was paying the least bit of attention to us. I couldn't figure out who had yelled, and evidently neither could she. She shrugged her round, fleshy shoulders, and picked up right where she had left off. I could feel my impatience rising, as I wished her gone, and a moment later that same voice yelled, "GO AWAY!!!!"

This time, she huffed and glared first at me, and then at Tim. A moment later she waddled away from us with a pouty, angry expression.

I reached across and poked Tim, who shrugged and smiled. He then said, "Well, it worked didn't it?"

Yes, it had worked. Without uttering a sound, he had voiced what we were both feeling, and with enough force to make her leave. For the remainder of my stint in that horrible war room, he became my shield from both the noise and from unwanted guests.

Although the noise in the physical world can sometimes be unbearable, usually my shields (or blocks) keep it within a range I can ignore. While this can sound as if seeing, sensing, and knowing all this information is traumatic, it's important for my job.

In the astral plane, understanding and reading auras is extremely helpful. Being able to look at someone and instantly understand their emotional and mental state is often crucial. It can mean the difference between someone having a smooth and love-filled transition or a rough and fear-filled transition.

If I go to meet someone and I see that their aura is full of red and grays, and is spiky and drawn inward, then I know I need to let my aura flow outward and cover theirs. I need to envelope us both in a calming and soothing light that will allow them to move away from their physical form in a stress-free way.

Most times the light I cover them in is white or the palest of lavenders, indicating that I'm using my spiritual center to cloak us. But other times it can be green or golden indicating that it is coming from my emotional center. And in certain instances, I combine both.

Each situation is different, but I (and all the escorts and guides) try to give every soul what they need to make the transition as easy and love-filled as possible.

Emotions and Death

BECAUSE DEATH IS a very emotional time for everyone, each person's death (and the emotions surrounding it) greatly influence what they experience when they first transition.

If someone crosses over while calm and accepting of their death, then the transition is easy and relatively painless. However, if the person crosses over while depressed (perhaps having committed suicide), then the transition will be bleaker and more troubling. The same is true of someone who is angry about their death or angry with someone they are leaving behind.

For the person who has died, there is no longer a way for them to easily focus their emotions at the cause of their anguish or anger. This creates an emotional block around them. Emotional blocks make it difficult for escorts like me to smooth the way. So, the first thing we need to do is work with the person to help them release the emotion (anger, depression, fear) that they might be holding on to.

The more anger, fear, sadness, or other negative emotion that someone brings across, then the more calming and compassionate emotions we need to emit to nullify the emotional barriers around them. We need each person we transition to feel protected, safe, and loved. To that end, we need to create a loving, accepting, and calming atmosphere around them.

Any negativity that someone brings across affects not only the person generating it, but also all those around them in the transition level. And, if the negativity is strong enough, it can bleed through all the levels of the astral plane and affect every soul there. That is why it is so important for an escort or guide to be there when a person transitions. The escort helps each transitioner find their emotional balance. We help each soul realize where they are, and we help them understand what has happened.

Guides and escorts don't remain with a person forever, but we do remain with each person long enough to get them acclimated. That includes getting the environment stabilized and calmed, helping the soul understand (or remember) how to control their emotions, and aiding them to remember how to establish the type of environment or reality that they want to experience.

As an escort, I can transition someone (escort them across, adjust their reality to their expectations, work with them to help them understand where they are and what has occurred); however, if they are reluctant to acknowledge their new reality, then I need to pass them on to a guide. This is because as an escort, I'm limited. I cannot dedicate myself to each soul and their issues full time. Eventually, I need to return to my own physical body.

Escorts can do a lot, but we are human (corporeal), and our bodies do require that we attend to them – at least occasionally. That's why we usually work in tandem with a guide. If a soul requires more time than an escort can give them, then the guide can be there for them and the soul isn't left alone. This is especially important when the death is unplanned or unnatural.

Not All Deaths are Created Equal

WHEN SOMEONE DIES an unplanned or an unnatural death, a death caused by things like sudden violence (such as murder, vehicle accidents, bombings, tornadoes, hurricanes, and other acts of mayhem), it becomes particularly important for escorts and guides to act quickly.

Most of those who suffer such horrifying deaths are disoriented, confused, and unable to comprehend where they are. And while they need to be brought up to speed slowly and gently, they are often surrounding themselves in tumultuous and negative emotions, which are magnified in the astral plane. That means we need much more focus and energy output to help them, because we need to nullify their emotional output, while at the same time trying to help them acclimate to their new situation.

One such event occurred to me several years ago, when I was called in to help transition several victims of a violent school shooting. I came in unprepared (something I know better than to do, but I had been called in after having just finished with a different transition, and so wasn't fully prepared for the onslaught of raw emotions that awaited me when I arrived).

The horror, fear, and anguish flowed out of the victims and rolled over me like a tsunami. If a guide from my crew hadn't been there to work with me, I'm not sure I would have been able to do my job. That's how overpowering it was.

The guide touched my arm to reinforce the link between our energies. Once our energies merged, we had an easier time nullifying the effects of the trauma. This then made it simpler for us to quiet the miasma of emotional energies that were threatening to overload the area.

Working together, we eventually got the transitioning souls settled into their respective realities. Most returning souls remain within their private bubble of reality until they're ready to recognize that they are no longer physical. Once that realization takes hold, then the guides and counselors (and sometimes escorts, if we're available) begin the tasks of helping the souls integrate into life in the astral plane.

Most times one guide can watch over several of these bubble realities; but because this had been such an emotional crossing, we asked another guide from our crew to help. Therefore, two guides watched over our returning souls and waited for them to awaken to their new lives.

Part of Two Worlds

BEING AN ESCORT for the dead means being part of two worlds—the physical and the astral. I straddle the line between the two on all levels. In fact, none of the escorts (or at least none of those I know, anyway) ever fully let go of either reality...and probably won't until we die and move on ourselves. Until then, we remain part of both worlds.

I used to think it was quite novel, living in one reality and working in another. I mean, how many people do you know who do this? But now I've grown used to it and it just seems normal.

You commute to your job, and I commute to mine. Unlike you, though, I don't use conventional modes of transport to get there. (I mean, let's face it, most buses don't have a stop on the astral plane.)

When I'm on call or have a transitioner to meet, I just move my focus from my physical body, physical senses, and physical surroundings to my spiritual body and senses, and my astral surroundings. I do this via meditation, by focusing my energies fully on the astral plane (which allows me to just walk out of my body), or through lucid dreams.

While walking out of my body during a sleep cycle is the easiest and least disruptive to the physical form, it isn't always convenient. Some people can drop off to sleep no matter what time of day or night it is, but it's not that easy for me. So, if someone needs me during the middle of my day, then I need to *commute* using a different method other than sleep (I primarily use meditation).

(It's also interesting to note that those of us who commute during sleep cycles often incorporate our experiences into dreamlike events; however, unlike ordinary dreams, these dreams are memory remnants of actual events, so they don't fade like normal dreams would).

Of course, since I do maintain a life in the physical plane, which includes a job to which I travel by car, taking daytime gigs is difficult. The last thing I want to do is leave a soul without an escort, yet it's not always convenient to walk out of my body. (Can you imagine being in a conference room while giving a business presentation, and literally dropping everything to respond to someone's call? Not a good idea.) That's why most souls who are transitioning, create agreements with escorts and guides.

Creating Links

I MEET WITH different souls on the astral plane and we make agreements and arrangements for transitioning. This means creating links of energy between us. These links allow someone to call us when they need to go.

These links can be created at any time (while between lives, years before their death, or just hours before dying). However, since many people die of age-related issues, a lot of them wait until they are senior citizens to set things up with an escort.

Once the agreements are made, everyone goes about their daily lives, until the time comes for that agreement to be fulfilled. That's when the link is tugged or pulled. (That's the best explanation I can give for how it feels…like someone tugging on a small rope that I have tied around my body.)

Because the link is connected at the soul level, I instinctively know who is calling and where they are. I just need to let go of my physicality and go there. However, sometimes I need to let the caller know that their timing is off. Sometimes, I need to ask them to wait (if possible).

This is doable because the linking works both ways. By opening the link completely, the caller can instinctively hear me when I let them know that their timing is inconvenient. They can also sense where I am and what I am doing (at least in a vague way). They may not know that I'm at my office or at the zoo with my family, but they do know that I'm in my home region in my home country and they can (at the soul level) recognize that it may not be an optimal moment for me to come.

Therefore, the linking helps everyone. The person calling, can (if possible) arrange their death to coincide with when I can be available. And I can be aware that someone will need me soon.

Of course, that only works in the case of a slow death. Sudden deaths are totally different. If the call is for an unplanned or unnatural death and I can't be there, then I need to route the call to someone I know can cover for me. If I don't, then the links the caller and I forged when we made the agreement are still connected, and I end up getting the full brunt of their emotional anguish. So, it's always best to call for a stand-in if you can't make it.

If I'm making it sound as if people have a choice in their deaths, it's because they do (most times). Someone who is dying of an illness will often hold on until everything is settled—relatives have visited, disputes are reconciled (if possible), and (believe it or not) their escorts are ready to go. In fact, many times we escorts come and spend time with them prior to their departure, especially if it's a protracted illness.

Choosing When

Anya was six and she was dying of cancer. I and another of my crew spent a week standing by her bedside each night helping her come to terms with what was happening. We answered her questions, and she had a lot of them, especially during the long nights when she couldn't sleep. Was it hard to die? What would happen to her parents? What about her brother; would they (her family) be ok? Would she find her dog up there (he had died just the year before)? We were honest with her, and she was fine with our answers.

We also used our abilities to help her transcend the intense pain that she was dealing with. It was her desire to be coherent and brave for her family, and so she didn't want to take a lot of drugs for the pain. During her family's visits, she tried to tell them about us, the angels that were watching over her, but (of course) they accepted it as just side effects of her many medications.

Anya knew when it was time to let go, she understood that her body could no longer sustain her soul and she needed to leave. She gently tugged on the cord, but when I didn't respond right away, she modified her plans.

She could have left. Another member of my crew was

with her. However, she waited through the day, periodically checking with me via our connection. When I was finally able to come to her, I did.

I got there several hours after her initial call, and by her smile I knew she was glad to see me. A moment later, she let go and we all crossed over. She could have easily let go and just gone ahead without me, but it was her choice to wait for me. She wanted me to be there with her, and I was…eventually.

As an interesting side note to this story, several years later when I began volunteering at one of the local hospitals, I was given a tour of the facility. As I walked into the children's oncology area, a young girl of about nine ran up and hugged me. Her mother was a bit startled by her daughter's familiarity with this unknown (to them) person. So, when she asked her daughter why she felt the need to hug me, her daughter told her that I was the angel lady who had taken her friend Anya to heaven three years before.

This little girl had shared a room with Anya and had seen me and my crew member during our vigil in Anya's room. However, her mother, like Anya's parents, had never quite believed the stories of the angels that were watching over her friend. What this girl's mother made of me and her daughter's story, I'm not sure because I never saw them again after that tour.

However, it's good to note that being recognized like that is a rare occurrence. That's because most times we don't look like ourselves when we're on the job; most of the time we adjust our appearance to fit whatever expectations the transitioner has. Many people expect someone out of their own life, such as their spouse, father, mother, aunt, uncle, grandparent, sibling, friend, or (sometimes) even their long-gone pet to come and get them when they cross over. Others expect some sort of religious figure to come for them.

While souls of relatives and friends will come, if they can, it's not always possible. Often, it's been years, maybe even decades, since these people have died, and they've moved on to other tasks or other lives (yes, I mean reincarnated). Therefore, escorts or guides are called in to fulfill the request and meet the dying person's expectations.

In this case, though, Anya didn't really have any specific expectations, which is quite rare. So, both my crew member and I had retained our own physical images (more or less) while in the spiritual form.

Usually, it doesn't matter who we look like, since it's often only the person who is dying who sees us. And if others do see us (and it does happen), the sightings are typically put down to fatigue, stress, indigestion, or hallucination. It's rare that anyone other than the person we come to transition understands or acknowledges our presence.

Most occurrences of an accidental sighting (that is, when someone other than the person we're there to escort sees us) occur in hospitals or hospices. I attribute this to the fact that most hospice and hospital workers are slightly more aware because they deal with and cope with death so often. They've come to recognize the nuances of life and death, and many of them are as adept at seeing around corners as those they care for.

It's the same for many of the patients. They've come face to face with their own mortality and it has left them more aware of their surroundings. You add that to some of the medications these patients receive, and the walls of personality they usually have around them fade, allowing them to see us when we visit.

No Agreement? No Problem

CREATING AGREEMENTS WITH an escort is an option. That means that there are also a lot of people who decide to go it alone. While most of them find their way to the astral plane just fine when they die, others can get lost or not even realize that they have died. So, even those without agreements can require our services.

That's where the generic link comes in. This is a cord that links each escort to a guide. That way, if a guide needs one of us to respond to a situation (one or two lost souls), the guide can call us into service to help.

This same cord also enables the guides to call a group of escorts when a disaster in the physical world occurs.

Death in an Earthquake

I don't work every night. I can go weeks or months without getting a call, and then I'll get as many as four or five in a night. It's all relative. There are also times when the whole crew is called up because of some regional disaster. If it's a huge disaster, like a major earthquake with accompanying tsunami, then many crews might be called out.

I answered just such a call one night. When the call came, I had no idea what was wrong. One minute I was sleeping soundly in my bed, and the next I was standing in a meeting area of the astral plane.

Dressed in my usual white outfit, I wandered in the direction of our unofficial leader (the oldest member of our crew) to find out what was going on. The area was unusually crowded, and it took me a moment before I realized that there were at least a dozen other crews there. Everyone seemed extraordinarily hushed and I wondered what we were waiting for.

When I reached my crew leader, a whitening glow began at one edge of the room. It flowed across the crowd and as the white light filled my eyes, images flooded my mind.

I saw a large wave sweeping across the land, followed by the image of a map. I now knew why so many of us had been called in. With a destination firm in my mind, I blinked out from the astral plane and reappeared in the bottom of a collapsed building.

In front of me was a boy, who looked to be about 10 or 11, trapped in a corner of the basement. The building had collapsed inward, taking the boy with it. Now most of the debris seemed to be piled on top of him.

My light, the light of my soul, was the only illumination, and it cast a pale blue-white glow over the devastation. As I floated into the area near the boy,

I saw no movement, and I thought I might have arrived too late.

If the boy was already dead, his soul might have departed and gotten lost. (If someone dies without one of us to help them, they can sometimes wander the physical world confused and unsure of what they are supposed to do or where they are to go. This is more prone to occur during unplanned deaths—accidents and natural disasters.)

However, my illumination must have aroused him because I saw his deep brown eyes open slowly. His broken body was twisted as badly as the wreckage that buried him, and a small whimper of pain escaped him as he reached out to touch me.

"Are you an angel?" he whispered.

One of the odd things about being an escort is that when someone speaks to you, you can understand them perfectly no matter what language they speak. Also, when you answer, if you do, they understand you.

Because the boy expected angels that is how he saw me—a glowing light-being with a slightly female shape, yeah, I guess you could call that an angel. I nodded, and he smiled and closed his eyes. A moment later, he opened them again, and I caught the slight glisten of tears reflected in them.

"Will you take me to heaven to see my baby sister?"

I nodded again. After all, if that was what he wanted, then that is what I would provide him with—it is what I do, after all.

The wait wasn't long, and yet it was interminable. I hovered nearby, extending my energy around him to lend whatever comfort to him that I could. The boy reached out a tentative hand to touch me and I took his hand. However, I also saw Death standing off to the boy's other side. As the boy grew weaker, the image of Death grew stronger. This was his own belief system at work. He felt somehow in his mind that Death was stealing his life force, so he saw Death growing brighter and stronger, while he himself grew weaker.

Quietly and gently, the boy's body ceased functioning, and the boy stepped out, his hand still holding onto mine. At the same time, Death faded back into the blackness of the basement, his job complete.

The boy and I walked toward a brightly lit doorway. Through my contact with the boy's soul, I read his needs and expectations, and in the nanosecond that it took to move from this world through the doorway of light and into the astral plane, I had established a small apartment—his home when he was alive—filled with his family and friends. They were all there, waiting for him, even his baby sister who had died earlier.

As we walked into the room, he dropped my hand and rushed forward into the embraces of his friends and family. I could feel tears welling up in my own eyes, and I turned away from the scene. It seemed so unfair. He was just a kid.

There were several more similar events that night as we made sure that all of those caught in the disaster were taken care of.

Nights like that are hard, and in the mornings, I usually wake up feeling as depleted and run down as if suffering from the flu. Luckily though, that type of disaster doesn't occur too often. However, when things like that do happen, I know I'll go, because I can't even imagine not being there for someone.

Other Lives (or Deaths) I've Touched

I'VE TOUCHED MANY lives and escorted many souls on their journey to the afterlife. These are just a few of my memories that I would like to share with you.

Reliving Happy Memories

Recently, I escorted Betty across. She wasn't as old as she looked. She had stomach cancer and was in a great deal of pain, and that had aged her prematurely.

When she called me, I went to her. As I floated into her hospital room, she was sleepy and not too happy about being awakened. I reached down and took Betty's hand and we floated out of the room and into the astral plane.

Betty, who before had lain crumpled on a hospital bed, wasted, old, and emaciated, now stood next to me a healthy and smiling younger woman. Her hair was light brown, softly curled, and her eyes shone with loving happiness.

A glow of remembrance surrounded her as she looked

at the rambling, gray, frame house that now stood in front of us. We walked toward the large memorial garden that had been planted in the front yard, and she stooped to touch one of the white stones that outlined the heart-shaped garden. A profusion of flowers in jelly-bean colors was planted throughout the garden. In the center was a simple white, stone marker.

A figure in black stood nearby, and I realized that her fear of death was being brought forward. However, other than standing near the garden and looking slightly menacing in his black attire, there wasn't much to her vision of Death.

Her energies shifted as she followed her memories down the path of her life now gone. I was letting her move us through the various scenes of her memory. (Many times, when a person transitions, they relive those moments of great happiness or sadness before finally moving on. In her case, she chose to relive some of her happiest memories.) I simply added the control needed to make these scenes real (at least to her).

We were now taking part in a beautiful wedding ceremony. A large barn-like structure was filled with people sitting on folding chairs, and sunlight spilled through openings up near the ceiling. Betty sat next to a construct of her husband, and they beamed up at the wedding couple—her daughter (played by me) and a construct of her son-in-law. Again, in the back row of wedding guests stood Death, but he seemed paler than before.

The minister finished the wedding ceremony, and we were surrounded by smiling, happy family all congratulating us. Then the woman came and gave me a hug, and the scene shifted around us again.

Now we were in a smaller, more suburban garage. Two bicycles stood near the back wall, leaning on their kickstands. A shine in her eyes and a huge smile on her face, Betty grabbed the red one and flung her leg over it. She used her heel to push the kickstand out of the way, then she waved to us—her daughter (me), and the constructs of her husband and son-in-law— and rode out into the sunlight.

She pedaled slowly down the driveway toward the tree-lined street, calling over her shoulder for her husband to hurry up.

A moment later, the construct of her husband pulled on a helmet, and smiled at me. Then he, too, pedaled out of the garage and down the street.

I looked at Death, standing in the corner of the garage, and realized that he was very ghostlike now. That meant she was almost over her fear of being here. Smiling to myself at how well she was adapting, I left knowing that the guides would take loving care of her.

Flying Home

Harvey was an accountant who always wanted to be a pilot. He even went so far as to take a few lessons, but

then stopped when his mother declared it too
dangerous.

However, dangerous or not, he and I flew to heaven in
a single-engine Piper Cub.

He did loops and barrel rolls (and I managed not to get
sick, even though it felt very real). I must admit, even
for me, even knowing that I was the one creating the
experience for us, it was exhilarating and fun.

The only small planes I've ever been on are the little
puddle jumpers that took me and my hubby from the
mainland to some tropical islands. While not scary,
they also don't give you the same view as riding in the
co-pilot's seat. Seeing the world (real or construct)
through that large expanse of glass is stunning (even if
I do say so myself).

We spent hours (or so it seemed) flying through that
wide expanse of blue. The sun was blinding (almost as
blinding as viewing your own soul), and when it shone
through the fluffy, white clouds, a thousand mini-
rainbows appeared, sparkling like gemstones in the
sky.

A flock of birds flew alongside for a bit, and Harvey
commented how he felt as if he could simply leave the
plane and fly with them. (He could, but he didn't know
that.) He was so filled with joy; he was like a child in
his happiness. His grin was so infectious that I
couldn't help but smile back at him.

We flew over cities and towns, forests, and fields, and he was happy, deliriously, delightedly happy. Finally, he said he wanted to show me something, and he banked left to circle lower. I could read his energies, so knew where he wanted to be and what he expected to see and quickly made sure it was there for him.

We circled down to where he could point out his boyhood home (his sister lived there now with her husband and two kids, he told me shyly). He then pointed out his old alma mater (within those hallowed halls was where Beefy McMasters used to beat him up after school), the library (his favorite refuge from the bullies and his mother), and the apartment where his grandmother had lived.

He pulled up on the stick and headed toward downtown Manhattan. He again swooped low to point out certain sites. (Yes, I know it's strictly forbidden to fly over Manhattan in a little plane, but it was Harvey's wish, so we flew over Manhattan.)

He pointed out his office and his favorite coffee shop where the cute, little waitress worked; the one that he was working up the nerve to ask out. (He'd been working up the nerve now for two years.)

He then aimed the little plane toward the coast and headed north towards Maine. He was amazed at how easily he could handle the plane, and how well he knew what to do to control it—especially, he confessed, since he'd only finished a handful of lessons. He had been so sure that flying a plane would be much more difficult, but now he was glad to find out that it wasn't.

He prattled on while pointing at this and that as he cruised through the air with me sitting quietly in the co-pilot's seat. Then, after what seemed to him to be hours, but was really only moments, he asked where he should land. After all, he was sure that the plane must be nearly out of fuel since we had been flying for so long.

So, I created an astral version of the Teeterboro airport (Teeterboro, New Jersey) and pointed it out to him. Still grinning like a kid, he banked to land. He lined up everything perfectly and came in as gently as a feather (of course). He then taxied to the hangar that I pointed out to him.

As we climbed down from the plane, I explained that the hangar and the plane were his now, and he could take the plane anywhere he wanted to, for as long as he wanted to. With several hugs, and absolutely no dimming of that infectious grin of his, I walked away from the hangar.

As I left, I thought how interesting it was that he had never created an image of Death...we had had no other guests in the plane with us, nor did anyone join us at the airport. It was just the two of us from the moment I entered his quiet little condo in the Bronx, until I left him at the hangar. In fact, there had been no real fears, just a few regrets, that's all.

Motorcycle Gang

It was dark, and not just because it was midnight. No, there was another kind of darkness around this place; a darkness that hovered like a deadly gas, permeating the building and the area around it. I didn't want to be here, but someone had called me to this dingy roadside bar, so here I was.

Already I could feel the emotions from the people inside. They pummeled me like a sledge-hammer—hate, anger, fear, but mostly rage. It was a blood-letting, overpowering, kill-everything-in-sight rage. It was cold, too…not the temperature, but the feel of the energies.

I shuddered and pulled my energies closer to me as I tried my best to block out the overwhelming miasma of negativity that filled this place. Taking a couple of steps inside, I tried to figure out why I was there.

There were about 15 people standing along the walls staring at the three fighters in the middle of the room. The dress code seemed to be jeans and t-shirts, accessorized with biker logos, leather vests, and chains.

I noticed that several bodies already littered the floor, but whether they were dead or merely unconscious was a little more difficult to discern due to the overwhelming rage that filled the room. The source was a scruffy-looking young man over by the pool tables. Knife in one hand, and a broken pool cue in the other, he was holding off two others. A gun was on the floor, half under one of the pool tables near the body of a young woman.

I felt the brush of something even colder at my back, and when I turned around, I saw a tall biker standing behind me. He was dressed all in black leather with a chain wrapped around his waist, and another slung over his shoulder. The only face I saw was mine reflected in his black-visored helmet, but I knew it was Death, he just had that aura about him.

I heard the whooshing of air coming toward me, and a moment later a broken pool cue swept through where I was standing and collided with someone behind me. I spun around in time to see a guy in a red t-shirt collapse onto the dirty barroom floor his face an indistinguishable mess of blood and dirt.

A moment later, a shotgun blast filled the room, and suddenly there was silence. Yet the rage and hatred hadn't diminished, and the source of those emotions was now stalking toward me. No…it took me a moment to realize, he was stalking towards Death.

I backed up, stepping gingerly around the body of the guy in the red t-shirt. As I repositioned myself, I heard an odd rumbling sound, and looked around for the source. When I finally realized that Death was laughing, I couldn't stop the thought from forming, "…well, as long as he was enjoying himself."

A young woman then took my attention. She was

perhaps 19 or 20 and had moved away from the wall. She now stood staring at the body under the pool table and I watched her face as recognition streamed across it. When she opened her mouth to scream, I grabbed her hand and transitioned her to a construct of the bar.

I left her sitting on the floor next to a construct of her body, as I felt the link to the real bar pull me back there (evidently, I wasn't done yet).

I popped back into the bar, and Death and the rage-filled biker were dancing around each other, each with a knife in one hand, and a rather odd-looking chain wrapped around their other wrists. I puzzled about it for a moment, until I realized that another of the escorts who had responded to this call had locked them together because the young man still had no idea that the shotgun blast from a moment ago had literally torn him in two.

The young man's rage so consumed him that he was literally fighting against his own fears, which he had projected into this construct of Death.

Another young man was coming toward me now, and for a moment I nearly panicked. Then I realized that he was coming towards me because no one else could see him. He must have been the reason why I was pulled back here so strongly. I quickly grabbed his hand and took him across to the construct of the bar where the girl was.

Being in the construct greatly reduced the emotions I

had been dealing with, and I released some of the
tension that had wound itself around my own energies.
As I checked on the young woman, I saw she was still
hunched down next to the image of her body, but now
I could feel waves of regret and remorse pouring off
her.

She knew she was dead, so now it was time to move
her to a place where she could begin to deal with that
information. I gently touched her shoulder and moved
her to a construct of her childhood church. She wanted
comforting and forgiveness, and she had always found
them with her religion and her mother, so that's what I
gave her now.

Inside the church she found a construct of her mother,
and her favorite pastor. And when I left, they were
doing their best to console and comfort her.

Hoping a more neutral territory would make it much
easier for the rage-filled biker to calm and perhaps
come to terms with his situation, I hurried back to the
real bar. Death and the knife-wielding biker were still
paired off, and laughter and swearing filled the air.
Death danced around the biker, causing the chains he
wore to rattle, while they each swung at each other
with their knives. Small cuts and slices decorated the
biker's arms, legs, torso, and face, yet Death was
untouched.

I reached out and placed a hand on the biker's
shoulder. As we arrived in the astral plane, I quickly
retreated, but it was if I hadn't been there. His focus

never left his creation of Death. The red energies around them buzzed like high tension wires. Sickened, I looked away.

The other young man I had left here was now sitting at one of the tables, his head and face buried in his hands. His energies and his posture told me he was ready to move on to his own reality, and a brief touch told me what to create.

Within moments we were away from the bar and at the funeral home where his family was gathering. Though not entirely sorry for the life he had picked, he was sorry that he had hurt his family by not becoming the type of son they had wanted. I left him with the other escort who would sit with him during the funeral service. Once he was able to fully accept what had occurred and where he was, he would work with a guide to resolve the guilt and remorse he felt so it wouldn't necessary carry over into his next life.

Back at the astral bar, the rage still seethed around the room in a red and black swirl, filling the room like cigarette smoke; only more insidious and more dangerous. There was no telling how long they would keep fighting. Because as long as the biker continued to hoard his fears, angers, and jealousies, he would keep trying to fight Death or anyone else that crossed his path.

Shaking my head, I called in a guide to baby sit. There wasn't any more I could do. Now it was up to each person to come to terms with where they were and what had happened to them.

As I left, I kept seeing that sinuous snake of red and black energies in my mind, and I wondered how anyone could have that much hate and rage inside. It made me sad. I hoped that the biker would soon realize that he was in a place of love now, and so let go of that anger and rage.

Visitations

Some of those that crossover, do so after a brief stop to visit with someone important to them. Most times it is little more than a quick moment; a flash of energy that allows the living to see a likeness of the person who just died.

Sometimes, souls who have just crossed over and are still in the transition level will expand their energy enough to make their presence known when they see how upset their family and friends are at their death. Again, the moment is short, but it may be enough to help everyone through their mourning period.

For those whose family, friends, or loved ones are not intuitive enough to understand or perceive the visitations, it is sometimes necessary to contact someone who is. This may be someone who functions as a professional medium, or it may be a friend or acquaintance who is intuitive enough to perceive the visitation and pass along the message that the deceased needs their loved ones to receive.

Most times the messages are simple: they (the deceased) are fine; they are in a good or happy place; they are with others who share the love; and they want us (the living) to be happy, too. There is no place for guilt, grudges, or shame, in their world. They want us to understand that life continues, even after the body dies. And they want us to understand that the spiritual world is one of happiness and peace.

I have personally received a number of such visitations. Some occurred when I was a child or tweenager (my uncle and my grandparents), and several visitations happened while I was debating with myself about writing and publishing this book. Both of these visitors encouraged me to keep going because they felt that what I had to say was important.

However, I have also escorted those who wished to make a stop or two on their way Home.

Encouragement

Sometimes souls stop by to help those left behind. I had been struggling with the best way to present the information for this book. I'd write several chapters, and then throw them out. I just couldn't seem to find my voice for this project.

As I struggled with this book, a good friend of mine died, but I didn't know that. We lived on different continents, so communicated electronically most of the time. And she'd not told anyone she was ill.

So, imagine my surprise when I looked up from my

writing to see her smiling at me from the doorway to my office. Amazed and pleased, I scrambled to my feet, and ran over to give her a hug. However, when I reached for her, she put a hand up to stop me. Puzzled, I simply stared at her, a huge grin on my face. I asked her when she had arrived, but she didn't answer.

I then directed her to the chair by my desk, and she shook her head. That's when I saw her image waver. As often as I had dealt with the dead and dying, I hadn't realized that she was noncorporeal. Tears started running down my cheeks, and that's when I heard her say, "Just be honest. Write from your heart."

She reached out to touch my cheek and her image faded away. Several hours later, I got a phone call from her sister notifying me of my friend's death.

Evidently, she wanted me to write the book and so stopped by to give me the advice and encouragement I needed to do so. (And no, just because I'm friends with someone doesn't mean that I'm their escort of choice. Oftentimes, that is just too difficult for both the dying person and the escort.)

A Goodbye Hug

I met Mary in her hospital room. Her heart had been unable to support her body anymore, so she had decided to leave. As I reached out my hand to help her cross over, she suddenly became coy. She told me she needed to make some stops before leaving, and I nodded.

Holding her hand, I let her direct us to the people she wanted to see. I merely added the impetus and control since she wasn't quite sure how to handle being out of her body yet.

The first place we appeared was a child's bedroom. Mary leaned over and smoothed back the bangs of her granddaughter (or at least she made the motions of doing so). Although unable to touch her granddaughter, the love from her soul enveloped the sleeping girl and we both knew that on some level her granddaughter would know and understand that Mary had been there.

At our next stop, we popped into a foyer. There was a stairway leading up, a den or family room behind us, and a large kitchen in front of us. At the kitchen table were six rather subdued adults sitting and talking quietly.

As we appeared, the conversation stopped, and everyone turned to look into the foyer. Mary was using our combined energy to make herself completely visible; not misty and ghostlike, but solid and very real looking. (This is something you're not really supposed to do.)

She crooked her finger and one of the ladies at the table ran to hug her. Within moments all six adults were crowding around her hugging and crying and trying to find out how she had gotten there. However, the young lady who had first come over to hug her seemed to understand. Mary and the young lady nodded at each other in complete understanding. I urged Mary to conclude her visit, as my own energy was beginning to wane.

Mary had pulled so much of my energy to make herself visible, that I needed to finish my task quickly and return to my own body. She gave her daughter one last hug, and we transitioned to the astral plane.

I established the reality she expected to find in her version of the afterlife. Then, as soon as it was complete, one of the guides from my crew took over so I could return home.

While it might be dangerous to me to let someone draw on my energies like that, I also know how hard it can be to say goodbye. So, yes, I admit it...I'm a big softy. (But don't tell my boss, okay?)

Not Dead Yet

Sometimes, I escort people across who aren't dead, but who need to work out issues or reconcile with someone who has passed on. This entails coordinating a meeting with the soul who is in the afterlife, and then escorting the corporeal soul across.

Not all souls need assistance with this. Some souls are very adept at coping in the astral plane. However, those souls who are overly attached to the physical plane can be extremely uncomfortable separating from their physical forms, even while sleeping, and so request assistance.

Working on Issues

Chard wanted someone to help him cross over to meet with his wife who had recently died. This wasn't a request from the corporeal man; this was a request made at the soul level.

My crew leader asked me to meet with Chard, who had appeared in the transition level several times evidently looking for someone or something. I was told that when Chard appeared, he was frightened, lost, and unable to control his surroundings. The last attempt to help him had failed when he had unexpectedly jumped himself back to his sleeping body. However, they had gleaned enough information from touching his soul's aura that I could locate Chard in the physical plane, rather than waiting for him to appear again in the astral plane.

In spiritual form, I entered Chard's residence. When his soul sensed me, he came out. He said that he was trying to locate his wife who had just recently died. Their parting had been fraught with unresolved issues, and he really needed to speak to her (in person, as it were).

I told him I would arrange things, and for him to wait for my return. I transitioned to the astral and followed the mental image of his wife that he had given me. When I found her, she was quite willing to meet, so I went back for Chard.

We approached a large colonial-style house, like the one in which Chard lived in the physical plane. I knew that seeing this structure would make him more comfortable. We entered through the front doors, and from the grand foyer we climbed the curving staircase.

At the top of the stairs, he turned left and entered a large master bedroom suite. The soul of his wife was there, looking (I presumed) as she had in life. A delicate woman with red hair, she gave him a cold penetrating stare. There was a suitcase on the bed, and it looked as if his wife had been packing to leave.

She asked me to wait out in the hall, and I did as she asked. As I paced the hallway, I heard slamming drawers along with raised voices cajoling and pleading. I was wondering if I had made a mistake in bringing them together, when the arguing finally stopped. The silence stretched out and I worried about what might have happened in there, but finally the doors to the bedroom opened.

Both Chard and his wife were smiling, and the suitcase that had been open and half-filled on the bed was now nowhere in sight. Chard told me that everything was all right now; that he and his wife had worked things out. She had forgiven him, so he was now okay to go home. His wife nodded at me, and I smiled at them both.

I crossed Chard back to the physical world, where he rejoined his sleeping body, glad that he'd been able to get the closure he needed.

Staying and Going

Occasionally, I get called in unexpectedly. When that happens, all I can do is try to think fast and hope I can figure out why I'm there and respond accordingly.

It doesn't happen often (thank goodness). When it does, it's primarily during unexpected events or events involving large groups.

The Toy Store

When I got called the pull was immediate. One minute I was curled up in a chair reading a book and the next I was in a room with a lot of fluorescent lighting. There was an extensive supply of large pillows in oranges, purples, and greens scattered across the floor, and an overabundance of shelves with board games, bats, balls of all sizes and types, and mountains of stuffed creatures.

I stepped around several stuffed animals taller than I was and looked for someone to tell me why I was here. However, I seemed to be all alone.

I heard a child's whimper, and the next thing I knew I was covered in pink and white fur. I looked down and saw two elongated pink and white feet, two matching paws where my hands used to be, and yes…when I twisted around to look, there was a big fluffy tail on my butt.

When I straightened up, I reached for the top of my head. I could feel two long furry ears sticking up. I was sure if I looked in a mirror, I would have the face of a bunny, too

At least now I knew where I was; I was on the astral plane. I just wasn't sure why. A moment later a brown-haired girl of about two or three tugged at my hand (paw?). Her round, taffy-colored eyes were swimming in tears and her bottom lip quivered. She had a pink and white stuffed bunny clutched in her free hand, so at least now I knew where the bunny theme had come from.

"I can't find my mommy." Her bottom lip scrunched up and the tears rolled down her chubby cheeks.

I stooped down and picked her up. I let her cry, while mouthing soothing phrases. As I cooed and shushed, her crying finally subsided a bit.

I focused on the energies flowing around us and saw a silver beam of light sprouting from the top of her head. The light disappeared into the depths of the toy store. I told her to hang on tight, and she swung her stuffed rabbit around behind me and locked her hands together behind my neck.

I reached my hand out and touched the light beam. In an instant, she and I were pulled forward into an intense blue-white glow. The light flowed through us and around us, and we flowed through the light. At one point, it even felt as if we were the light.

With a jolt, we landed in a world of mist and moans.
As the fog shifted and swirled, an island of crumpled
and compressed cars and trucks was revealed, and then
hidden. I heard sirens, but they were still some
distance away. A horn was blaring, seemingly stuck in
the on position, and a weak voice cried for help.

The silver light led me through the maze of cars until I
stood next to a maroon sedan. The front end was
buried under a blue pickup, while an RV compressed
the back. A young woman, probably her mother, was
just beginning to stir in the front seat, and in the back,
snug in her car seat was my pink rabbit girl...the
physical version of her anyway.

It appeared that she had been visiting the astral plane
to avoid the emotional and physical pain of the
accident. Now we were back in the real world, and I
wasn't quite sure how to explain this whole experience
to her. I could tell her it was a dream, but I disliked
misleading people that way.

Sirens whooped nearby. Help was almost here.

I looked into her tawny eyes, and tried to make my
mouth work, but she beat me too it. "Is my mommy
going to be okay?" She stared at the woman in the
front of the crumpled sedan.

"I don't know," and it was the truth. I really didn't
know. I hadn't been contacted about this incident, so I
had no idea who was transitioning and who wasn't.

A group of emergency medical techs arrived, and the little girl became more interested in them and what they were doing than in any explanations or answers I might offer. I carried her over to the side of road where she could see what was happening, but where we were both out of the way.

The woman in the front of the maroon car began to respond to the EMTs treatments, and I breathed out a silent sigh. Meanwhile, one of the EMTs opened the passenger door to the maroon car and eased the little girl's body onto a backboard. As the EMT applied braces and checked her vitals, she faded from my arms and the girl on the backboard stirred and moaned.

"She's coming around," the EMT called out to his companions.

Tea-Time in the Garden

In a blink, I was gone from the fog. I was now sitting in a white, wrought iron chair wearing a yellow-flowered, chintz dress, with white gloves, and a large, yellow hat that dipped over my left eye. The chair was in a beautiful English garden—I could smell roses, gardenias, and lilacs—and the elderly lady sitting opposite me pointed to the silver tray on the matching white table and asked me if I wanted milk in my tea.

The look on my face must have shown my confusion because she asked me again, and I dumbly nodded. She dropped a dollop of milk into the thin porcelain teacup and smiled. Her hands were quick and agile, and her silvery hair was coiled up and covered by an elaborate lavender picture hat. The color of the hat matched the suit she wore, and on the lace ruff at the neck of her blouse, was a gorgeous cameo.

She held out one of the cups sitting on a matching saucer, and I thanked her as I took it and set in on the table in front of me.

"I do so wish you could have been here when Robert was alive," my hostess commented. "He had such a talent with the gardens." She took a sip of tea and smiled wistfully while glancing around at the colorfully blooming displays.

As she prattled on about her life and her lost love, Robert, I scanned the sky and fiddled with the linen napkin in my lap. I was hoping for some message— sky writing, a dove with a letter tied to its foot, maybe even a secret message written on the napkin in my lap—something that might tell me why I was here. However, when none of that occurred, all I could do was hope that her stories might give me some clue.

So, we sipped tea and nibbled cookies, and I nodded when it seemed appropriate, while I waited for some insight or inspiration. Suddenly, her eyes widened, and the cookie fell to her lap. She clutched at her throat, and her face reddened. I dropped my teacup onto the grass and sprang to my feet.

I raced over to the woman and tried to get her to stand.

Her mouth opened and closed several times, but no air was getting to her. Her eyes were rolling wildly, and she flopped out of the chair and collapsed on the ground. It had been years since my first aid classes, and I couldn't remember if I should roll her onto her side or make her sit upright.

The garden image dimmed; then returned; then dimmed again. I saw tendrils of fog swirling around an island of broken cars. We were back at the accident scene.

A man's voice cried out, "We're losing her." Another voice spoke, "There's something blocking her airway…"

The fingers of fog ghosted aside, and I saw my picture-hat lady's body being attended to by several EMTs.

The fog closed over the scene again, like curtains closing on a play, and I heard one of the EMTs state, "We lost her."

We were back in the garden, sitting at the table. All the tea things were back in place and it looked as if nothing untoward had happened. She was regaling me with some story about Robert again when her eyes came alive. Her whole face lit up and she joggled her cup into the saucer.

Her eyes were focused somewhere over my right shoulder, and she sloshed some of the tea out of the cup as she put the cup and saucer down on the table.

"Robert? Oh my…" her gloved hands fluttered to her face, "is it really you?"

A well-dressed older gentleman came around from behind me and joined us. The lady in lavender was on her feet, her arms held wide as the man she called Robert swept her up in a bear hug. When they finally parted, the man nodded to me and thanked me for coming.

"Did you need a ride back to town?" he inquired, his arm securely around the woman's waist.

I shook my head. Smiling, they turned and walked toward the manor house that was now visible. I did a quick look around to make sure everything was good, and I went back home.

The 7 Secrets of Life

MANY PEOPLE WHO have reported NDEs have also stated how their perceptions and outlooks toward life have changed. When I compiled these comments, I found a consistent theme in their current principles (tenets and beliefs).

Almost all of those with positive NDEs now had principles that echoed those that I had known internally since I was old enough to put coherent thoughts together.

These are real, every day (normal) people—not gurus or mediums, yet each of us has the same message we carry around inside.

However, I would like to share the message and the principles with everyone. Just because you haven't had an NDE, doesn't mean you can't experience what we have: an awakening, an epiphany of the soul.

So, here are the seven secrets of life that NDE-ers have learned:

1. **Everything is Choice.** Before we incarnate in physical form we plan and choose our

lives. We select our families, friends, potential mates, experiences, and challenges. We also choose where and when we'll be born (what socio-economic and political climate and circumstances). And after we're born, we continue to make choices that affect us and those around us.

2. **Everything is Connected.** Everyone incarnate and discarnate is connected. And we're all connected to everything—animate and inanimate. We all share the same base structure, the same energy base; therefore, anything we do affects everything and everyone else around us.

3. **Everything Needs Balance.** This is sometimes called karma, but it all comes down to learning to find the balance between our needs and our wants (or our "what we think we need"), between love and fear. The balance point is acceptance and tolerance, but there is a whole range of experiences between love and fear or need and want. (And acceptance is not the same as resignation—acceptance is full of love, while resignation is without hope and contains fear.)

4. **Life is Eternal.** Sentience never dies. The body we think of as ourselves will die, but the true being inside of that body does not.

The true body, the true us, lives forever.

5. **Life is Relationships.** Life is about the relationships we have with everything— our parents, ourselves, our jobs, our friends, our things, our pets, all of what we call nature, people we barely know (mail carriers, cashiers, neighbors, taxi drivers, etc.), other countries, religions, etc. How we treat ourselves and others is particularly important, because as stated earlier, we're all connected.

6. **Life is About Experience.** Knowledge, learning, and experience are important parts to life. Every time you choose a physical life you gain knowledge and experiences, and that contributes to your overall learning. Your overall knowledge contributes to the overall experiences of everyone else because we all learn from each other.

7. **There is a Unifying Power.** There is a unifying power, a super energy, a oneness, a singularity that binds us all together. Some of us call it God, some call it The All, and others call it a Supreme Being. Whatever name we give it, most people, especially those who have had an NDE are certain that it exists, even if they had been atheists prior to their NDE.

These seven principles seem to come through in the messages of loving acceptance that each NDE-er has. And these are the same seven principles that I have felt guiding my life since forever.

I must admit, I find it fascinating, comforting, and a bit satisfying to hear other "normal" people express these same seven secrets that I've been carrying around all my life. (I think it always makes you feel better when someone else can validate you or your beliefs.)

So, while I can't prove (in any scientific way, anyway) that these are the seven driving forces behind the world we live in, they have definitely been the seven driving forces behind my own life.

Expanded Perceptions

PEOPLE OFTEN ASK how I do what I do—see auras, read people's energies, or move between planes—and the answer I usually give is that I shift my perspective, I shift my focus.

For instance, when you look at the image below, what do you see?

Is it a tree with two birds flying overhead, or the faces of two animals?

Now, if you shift your perspective, what do you see?

Gestalt Theory says that the connections between everything creates a pattern that cannot be seen when viewed as independent parts. It also points out that the human mind perceives specific patterns and associates those patterns with the reality in which it exists.

So, if the two animals make up our perception of our current reality, then what happens if we shift our focus and no longer see the animals? What happens if we shift our perception and the pattern we see is now the tree?

It doesn't mean that the first reality wasn't real, nor does it mean the second one isn't real. They can both be real, especially if you consider that maybe the tree and the two faces aren't the complete picture. Maybe, they're just pieces to the whole.

Doing what I do means having an incredibly open mind as to what is real. I'm not talking about belief, but about acceptance, which is the absence of fear.

Belief says that I'm taking it on faith with nothing to back it up, and with the fear that someone might come along and prove me wrong. Acceptance says that I have some proof, though maybe not enough to convince a scientist, and that I'm not afraid of encountering another (differing) opinion or proofs. I'm also not afraid that what I'm experiencing contradicts my own internal truths. I'm open to the experience no matter what.

This is difficult for most people. Most people have a set pattern for how they view the world and they don't want anything to disturb that pattern. They're comfortable and happy just seeing the tree.

Other people, while comfortable and happy seeing a tree, don't mind a glimpse or two of the two animal faces, but they don't want it to happen very often or for very long. When it does happen, they can easily write it off as a dream, an hallucination, or some other acceptable anomaly.

Then there are those who not only don't mind seeing the two animal faces, but relish the opportunity to expand their horizons; to view the world through a new perspective, to see more patterns and try to figure out how they contribute to the whole.

To do what I do (to see the hidden parts of this shared reality), you need to lose the fear, and shift your perspective. Look for the two animal faces rather than the tree.

Lose the preconceptions you have as to what and how the world works. Expand the boundaries that you try to place around your thoughts. Once you do, you'll realize that the patterns you accept as part of your world aren't complete and that they have more parts to them. You must understand that the world you perceive through your five senses needs to include those parts that only your mind can perceive, too.

Gestalt is about perceiving patterns, and those patterns change based on how you view your reality. So, those unwilling or unable to shift their perceptions will always see the tree, while the rest of us will shift between the tree and the two animals.

The first time most people see beyond the surface of our own shared reality they blink, they turn away, and they wonder if it's real. But every time they look back, they keep seeing it.

Even those who are frightened by this new awareness continue to see it, at least until they can convince their minds to ignore it. Then, if and until someone points it out to them again, they will be blind to it because it doesn't fit with those patterns they consider normal.

But each time we see one of these patterns, we expand our perceptions. Each time we expand our perceptions, we realize how much more there is to our world, to our life, to our reality. And if we continue to look without fear at this world of ours, we may find even more "hidden" patterns.

Dreams or Memories?

THROUGHOUT MY LIFE I've encountered people who regard my assertions of my mostly nocturnal activities as flights of fancy or outright craziness. Other folks have asked me how I can be so positive that these activities are real and not just dreams, nightmares, or something happening simply in my mind.

My response is usually, "I find the reality of these incidents much more real than this world in which I'm speaking to you."

Think about your dreams for a moment (or can you even remember any of them?). Maybe you only remember a snippet here or a fragment there, right?

Dreams usually fade quickly. And although the most vivid dreams might leave you with a few vestiges of something vague and haunting, maybe a memory of an emotion or a smell, even those fade within a couple of days.

Dreams don't linger for long once you awaken, and nightmares are no different. Turn on a light, and nightmares inevitably run away, much preferring the dark recesses of your mind than the bright lights and activity of daytime.

These incidents of mine that I have just written about don't disappear once I awaken, and they don't scatter like rose petals from a dying bouquet. Instead, they're more like memories, which do fade, yes, but only after weeks, months, or years, not moments or hours. And like memories, some of my experiences as an escort can be retriggered by a smell, a word or phrase, a sound, or even by a color or image.

Dreams don't do that; not even memories of dream can do that. There's a certain musical phrase from Rhapsody in Blue that gives me a flashback to a jazz club and the pianist there who died while playing that tune. It was hours past closing time, but he was enjoying himself and entertaining the wait and cleaning staff when he died.

Then there is the smell of jasmine that recalls the memory of a young lady murdered outside her apartment in North Carolina. It's not a pleasant memory, and to this day, I'm no longer fond of the scent of jasmine.

These sounds, these smells trigger an emotional response, one that I associate with specific incidents, people, and places. That's what memories are— triggers to emotional incidents that we catalog and store. And when I'm acting as an escort, my emotional chakra is more open than when I'm functioning as a normal physical being. Emotions make strong memories, stronger than anything else.

Think about it for a moment. Bring up any memory—happy or sad, good or bad—and you'll find that the main thing you remember is the emotions of those involved. Perhaps you had an argument with your lover. You may not remember what was said, or even who started it, but what you remember is how you felt and how your lover felt.

Maybe you remember the first time you saw a kitten or a puppy. But again, what do you really remember? Do you remember exactly what the kitten or puppy looked like? No, but you remember how you felt…you remember the gooey, oh-so-loving, just-wanna-cuddle-you-to-death feelings that threatened to overflow your whole being.

So, while I may not be able to bring back something tangible that I can point to and say "There, see I was really there. It really happened," I do have memories.

I may not be able to prove to the skeptics that what I do is real, but when it's their time to leave, I'm sure they'll be glad to see me, or someone like me—even if we're not real.

The Spirituality of Death

ACCORDING TO THE American Journal of Psychology, somewhere in the mid-1800s death and all mentions of dying became taboo as spirituality was shunted aside and science began ruling the medical world.

However, as Western society again embraces spirituality and metaphysics, the way the medical profession handles things is shifting again. Spirituality is now being welcomed back into those realms where once only science was allowed.

Of course, not every physician is willing to change. That means many of them still follow the five unwritten rules regarding death and dying and discussions of same.

1. Avoid taboo topics such as the patient's appearance, future, upcoming holidays, or medications and treatments.

2. Stop discussing the current topic immediately if anyone in the room becomes emotional and add the topic to the list of those that are taboo (at least for that patient).

3. If the patient, patient's friend, or patient's
    relative mentions death or questions whether
    they or the patient is terminal, change the topic
    or leave the room.

4. Maintain normalcy always. Keep all
    conversations to a minimum and only discuss
    those things associated with normal healthy
    patients.

5. Be brief in all dealings with a terminal patient
    and their family.

However, many other people who work in the medical
profession are breaking free of those restraints.
Although, many medical people have been taught
Western philosophy and religions, many of them are
exploring other philosophies and seeking more
spirituality in their lives. This search is carrying over
into their careers, too.

And it isn't just the spirituality of life that they are
exploring; they are also beginning to explore the
spirituality of death.

Death is becoming less of a forbidden topic and more
of a curiosity and a challenge. People want to know
what it means to die. They also want to know whether
a soul truly exists, and if so, what happens to it when
the physical body dies.

People are no longer content to trust that heaven exists because some man in a pulpit says so. Instead, they're seeking "proof" or at least reassurances. They want something more than just the usual "…because I said so," responses to their questions.

People tend to believe in science and what it can prove; however, when it comes to life and death, neither science nor religion is enough. Many people are finding that there needs to be a blending of the two. That's where spirituality and metaphysics step in. These two are providing the basis for a unique way of looking at the world.

Science writes off NDEs as little more than biological and chemical reactions within a dying body. Religion claims they are glimpses of heaven (or hell). But, spirituality allows each person to interpret the event in their own way in accordance with their own needs. Meanwhile, metaphysics gives each event a sense of reality by grounding things in a scientific manner, yet, keeping an open mind for those things not easily explained.

Death is no longer the fear-filled event waiting for us at the end of our lives. Instead, death has become an intriguing question to which NDEs seem to hold the answers. Each reported NDE makes us feel as if we're a little closer to that answer. And each reported NDE draws people's attention to the questions of life, death, and the existence of a soul.

Many have rallied to the challenge of bringing death out of the shadows and into the light where it belongs, and once illuminated, it is impossible to ignore.

Even so, some doctors still view the dying as a personal failure, so will do anything to keep it from happening. They replace body parts; they hook the body to all manner of machines, tubes, and electrodes to keep it alive.

Eventually, though, even the doctors will have to recognize that life without death is a lie. It doesn't matter how many body parts you replace, or how many tubes or electrodes you attach to a person, when the spirit needs to leave, it will. That is how the circle of continuous life works.

Addendum: The Masters Speak

ONE OF THE truths that the masters like to stress is the fact that we do not cease to exist when our physical form dies. The concepts of life and death are only valid on the physical plane, and just part of the experiences we have all agreed to have.

We aren't a single flash or spark that simply dissipates once our body dies. On the contrary, we are more— much more—than just the shell we wear.

Life is Forever

From the masters: "When the body ceases to function, when the body ceases to exist, it has little impact on your existence. You are not your body. The physical form is little more than a means to an end.

"When you sleep you are closer to your true form/self, for when you sleep, you are then more in control and more able to leave the confines of the physical world. You can remove the focus from the physical plane without worry about

what might happen there and conduct the
business you need to in the other realities and
planes, of which you are a part.

"It is not that you are trapped within the physical
form, but only that you induce selective amnesia
while there. This causes you to forget that you
can leave anytime you want to, and it causes you
to forget that the physical form is not who you
are.

"Death is a concept that we do not share. We
create many forms and when we finish with these
forms, do we merge them back with us. So, there
is no death, there is only experience.

"You create for yourselves a world, a reality, and
then you populate that reality with forms you call
bodies and people. However, those forms are
you, and those realities yours, and when you
decide you have had enough of that form and
that reality, do you allow the form to cease
existence—or in your terms, die. The form, which
is energy from you, is reintegrated with you to be
re-used in another reality as another form; so, all
is continuous and everlasting. Nothing is ever lost
nor is anything ever extraneous. All is.

"Essence is eternal; it is only the physical form
that changes. When the lessons on this physical
plane are completed, then are lessons on the

astral arranged. However, a physical form is not manifested/created because on the astral a physical body is needed not.

"True life never dies; it never goes away. We are always one with each other, and we are always."

Forgetting Who We Truly Are

From the masters: "The fear of death is merely the fear of the unknown—or rather, the forgotten—because it is not so much unknown, as it is forgotten. It is only through the incarnation process that you have caused yourselves to forget.

"You create forgetfulness to more easily enjoy, join with, and participate in the various plays or scenarios you create for self once on the physical plane. Therefore, the concept of dying fills you with fear, for you suppose there is either some judgment or nothing, and both terrify you.

"However, there is not one who would judge, there is only you. You have chosen your life and you have chosen your death, so only you can decide whether to call the life successful.

"To us, all lives are successful, for all lives create experiences and all experiences add to the whole, which is all of us."

Life and Sentience

From the masters: "We are all alive, from the smallest element, to the All. Even those objects within your plane considered inanimate, are alive, but not all elements are sentient.

"We define sentience as having the capability of thought and change, while life is a state of being. All objects within the physical plane are alive because all things are made of us (all of us—you, us, the All...us), and we are alive. However, not all things are sentient, for sentient chairs or sentient clouds would gain little in terms of experience.

"Therefore, you exist in a state of life, but you are aware and knowledgeable, and capable of thought. While your leg is alive, it is neither aware nor capable of thought. So, your body is alive, but you (who are the body, the soul, and more) are sentient. You cannot die. The body can die, a chair can be destroyed, but you, the sentient being, cannot die nor be destroyed.

"An object is created from that which is you, but awareness is not there. The state of this object is alive. When the pattern of the object is rearranged, the object is destroyed or dead. The composition has not changed, but the pattern in which that composition was originally placed is changed.

"That you consider rocks as inanimate is true; yet
we see them as just as alive as any tree, or bird,
or shrub. Nor are rocks static or stagnant. They
erode, they crumble, they break, they roll and
shift positions, they may sink into the ground, or
fall down a mountainside. So, they too, are
constantly changing. There is no part of life that is
unchanging. All of life changes, grows, and shifts
because all is alive.

"Life and sentience are not the same. Although all
things are alive, only some [species] have the
awareness to recognize that they are alive and
that they can think, choose, and affect their own
lives.

"Rocks, wind, birds, and trees are alive, yet, they
have no awareness. They experience no thoughts,
and they make no choices, except those of basic
survival, whatever that might be for whatever
their species is.

"For granite, the basic survival does consist of
being. For a bird does survival consist of locating
and using those means of feeding and sheltering
self, as well as procreating. That this is also true of
trees is understood, for they, too, would seek for
food, shelter, and a chance to procreate. So
always is there life, and life with awareness
because all (things) are alive, but not all species

(within in your plane) are aware.

"Sentience can be rearranged in any form and is still aware. What you call death, we see as a variance in the energy patterns.

"We see the energies of what you call an apple in a particular pattern, a pattern indicating shape, size, color, taste. Therefore, when that apple's pattern is rearranged, you no longer see an apple, but we see the same energies only in a new structure or format. So, to us, nothing is ever lost, it merely changes.

"When you see the body stop moving or breathing, you envision the entire person as not living. However, we see the person as existing apart from the form rather than together. They have changed, but they have not ceased to be."

Transitioning

From the masters: "You look at physical life as a series of life experiences followed by a death. But the aging of the form and the eventual death of the form are just that—the death of the form.

"They are just part of the experiences gained on the physical plane, for the person is not dead. The person will take another form and gather more experiences.

Life to death = balance.
Young to old = balance.

"But these are transitions that you can experience
only in the physical plane. We do not age, for
there is no time and there is no form [where we
are], there is us and we are forever. There is no
death, for we are always aware. We can alter the
shape of what we call self, we can remove a
shape from play by placing it back within us, but it
is not dead, it is merely changed. Just as you, the
real you, do not die, but merely change.

"Most fragments upon the physical plane
associate the person with the form they see; thus,
do they presume that when the form is gone or
no longer functioning that the fragment is gone
and no longer functioning. But that is not a truth.
The fragment cannot die, it always is; it is merely
in a form or state not visible to the human or
cetacean eyes.

"Aging and death are just more anomalies of the
physical plane that those participating wished to
experience, for they occur nowhere else. Aging,
like time, is not available anywhere else. Without
the sense of time passing, can you not experience
that sense of aging.

"Death is merely the opposite of birth. That there

were nows (realities) in which birth and death were suspended from play is true, for those in that reality would experience life as one long drama, rather than a series of smaller or shorter ones. So, for them did the form not age, or if aging were required for the play, did it occur at a rate not noticeable to those within the normal time structures to which you are accustomed.

"That there are realities where the life of a form can last for thousands of your years is true, but it is the choice of those in that reality. Time, aging, and death are all just props in your set. You (all of you within your chosen reality) determine what the average life length is, what the average time flow is, even what the normal awareness level is. There is a lot to determining which now you will experience. Each [now] is designed to best help you experience those truths, those reactions, those lessons that you wish to. So many decisions go into the creation of your now."

Death and Life

From the masters: "You see death as an ending, but we, in essence, see life always. Death is a transitioning from one form of life to another—a transitioning from one life experience to another.

"You all fear what you do not know because your imaginations create all manner of objects, images, and ideas to fill that gap in knowledge. However, we give you something other than fear; we give you joy, love, and hope.

"We tell you that what you see as you is only a small portion of the real you. That the death of that small piece is not an end, but just an alteration in what is perceived (by you and by all those around you).

"Death is not an ending, nor is it something to fear. That is not to say that we encourage anyone to speed along their human death, nor do we encourage you to end the life prematurely. We mean that not at all. We merely indicate that you will find no demons, unless you so choose to, nor flames, nor devils, nor any other types of monsters, unless that is what you wish.

"Rather will you find an awareness so (to you) vast and all knowing that you will wonder how it is that you could have not realized all that you do now, then (then when you were still within that form, that body). The world is a vast and joyous place, and it extends way beyond your imaginings.

"Death is not full of pain unless you wish it to be; nor is it dark and cold, or within a void, or alone, or any of the other fears that you fill yourselves with.

"Death is a releasing of the focus, a releasing of the soul from that human form that no longer holds you. It allows the essence that is you to, like a butterfly emerging from its cocoon, take flight and soar.

"Death is a moving of focus from the narrow confinement of the physical plane, to the vaster and more expansive of all that you are. So, instead of fear, would we urge you to allow the joy and wonderment of the transition fill you.

"Those who would follow a great white light merely see their true self. They are the light. They are the brightness or the angel's choir or the incredible joy.

"They are remembering and experiencing again that freedom that is self; that widening perspective that allows them to see who and what they truly are. Therefore, depending upon their reliance on ego, they will see self, or they will see what ego wishes.

"Those who have left only to return [NDEs] have most often glimpsed that awareness of self (the bright light). The tunnel perceived is that narrow focus required for experiencing the physical realm.

"Some individuals make the transition easily, while some come to the astral with more difficulty. Rather than worry about death and one's reaction to it, would it be better to simply enjoy the life and all the experiences you have chosen, including that called death."

Glossary

I'm presenting a glossary of terms so you can more easily understand the information.

Abrading Energies: Most people's energy centers spin clockwise. Therefore, when they meet someone whose energy centers spin in a counterclockwise motion, the energies (or auras) abrade. There may only be two or three centers spinning in a motion counter to the person they're meeting, but even that can be enough to abrade.

This abrasion of energies can result in an instant feeling of dislike or discomfort when you meet. It is often referred to as "being rubbed the wrong way."

Acceptance: This is one of the seven goals. Its positive pole is agape, or unconditional love; its negative pole is ingratiation. It is used when you need a life emphasizing love and tolerance. This goal is common for fifth cycles (see Soul Cycles or Soul Age).

Active Center: It is one of the seven centers and is located at the thorax. Its positive pole is endurance; its negative pole is energetic (which is usually displayed in random movements such as pacing, gesturing, wiggling, tapping of the foot or fingers, or other physical outbursts of energy). (See Centers or Chakras)

Agape: This is a state of unconditional love for everything. This is considered the ultimate goal of all sentient physical plane evolution.

Aggression: This is one of the seven modes. Its positive pole is dynamism; its negative pole is belligerence. To be in aggression mode, means that you release your energy vigorously.

Agreement: An agreement is an understanding between souls (essences) or entities (a group of souls) to be or do some thing or to take some action. If someone agrees at the soul level to be available to support you when you need them, it means the two of you have made an agreement of support. If you agree to bear a child in which another soul would dwell, then you have agreed to be a mother. It doesn't mean you couldn't bear or create a child without an agreement, but it would be more difficult to become pregnant or to get someone pregnant.

But not all agreements are fulfilled. Sometimes, to fulfill an agreement, you would have to change your path or abrogate other goals, and this may not be agreeable; therefore, the agreement is abrogated instead. Also, monads and karmic bonds are more compelling than agreements, so you may have to let some agreements slide to complete a monad or work out an imbalance (karmic bond).

However, since agreements are more compelling than relationships without agreements, then when you meet someone with whom you have agreements, that person will hold your attention longer and your attraction to them will be stronger than with someone you have no agreements with.

Agreements are arrangements made between lives that offer aid, support, introductions, or other benefit. These are not binding, and they are not as compelling as imbalances (karmic debts) or shared lessons.

All: All That Is. Also called God, Yeshua, or the Tao. This is the awareness of being, the overall consciousness of sentience. It is the sentient energy from which all things were created—people, animals, the planet, light, heat, chairs, windows, everything. It is sometimes referred to as the Tao.

Arrogance: This is one of seven chief fears, or stumbling blocks, that a person chooses when they decide to become incarnate. Its positive pole is pride; its negative pole is vanity. It is a fear of being judged.

Artisan: This is one of the seven essence roles. The artisan seeks the structure and its realization. Artisans are often drawn to engineering, fine arts, genetic and botanical sciences, carpentry, all sorts of crafts, dance, or poetry. Many athletes are also artisans. The positive pole of the artisan is creation, the negative is artifice.

Astral Plane: This is one of the closest planes to our own physical plane. The focus of the astral plane is emotionalism. The frequency of this plane is faster than our own, so when we perceive images they are perceived as ghostly or gaseous vapors. There are seven levels or frequencies to this (and each) plane.

Attitude: This is one of the seven filters that we choose for each life. The attitude is a person's primary slant on life. The seven attitudes are stoic, spiritualist, skeptic, idealist, cynic, realist, and pragmatist.

Aura: This is the bubble of seven energies surrounding our physical body. These seven layers of energy are part of the true us, the spirit, the essence that is us. These energies, which come together to create the physical form we call a body, link us to the other six planes, as well as to the All.

Buddhic Plane: This is one of the faster vibrating planes. Its medium is pure or abstract kinetic energy. This is the plane next to the Messianic plane.

Cast: Cast is a reference to the vibrational pattern used in the physical plane. Certain portions of that pattern resonate at different frequencies. Dividing that pattern into seven positions indicates where within that frequency pattern you will find the vibrational frequency of each of the essence roles. Therefore, the server's vibrational pattern or frequency can (normally) be found in the fifth section of the overall pattern, and the scholar's in the fourth.

Causal Plane: On this plane the primary pursuit is the study of truth—individual truths, planal truths, dimensional truths, and pandimensional truths. Within the causal plane are the Akashic records, although most information relating to you and your past lives, current life, and future lives is also stored in your root chakra and instinctual center.

Caution: This is one of the seven modes. Its positive pole is deliberation; its negative pole is phobia. In caution mode, you release your energy carefully.

Centers: Another term for the chakras or energy centers distributed across your person. Each chakra, links one layer of your aura to your physical form.

Centering: Each person selects which center or centers that they will view the world through. There are seven centers: emotional, intellectual, spiritual, creative, interactive (communication), action, and instinctive.

A person's primary center is the dominant center that they use to experience life. The secondary center is usually the center through which the person responds. For instance, someone with a centering of the emotional part of the intellectual center will think about how they are feeling and try to describe those feelings instead of experiencing the emotions.

Chakra: One of seven major energy centers in the body. These are the primary connectors between your physical body and your essence. They also connect you to the seven planes of existence.

Chief fear: The chief fear is a person's primary obstacle, the focus of his fears and illusions. The seven chief fears are self-deprecation, arrogance, self-destruction, greed, martyrdom, impatience, and stubbornness.

Cording: The act of establishing a cord or connection with another person that either draws energy from them or adds energy to them. This can be done with or without the other person's permission. With their permission, the cording is done on the front of their aura; without their permission, the cording appears on the person's back.

Cords: The terms cords, links, and threads are similar and are many times used interchangeably. Cords can be agreed to or not. Those created without consent are usually found on the back of an energy center. For instance, if someone cords the back of your interactive center it is because they wish to monitor your communications or control what you say or do.

Cords or links of a more positive nature, such as those for agreements, lessons, or imbalances, can be found on the front of the energy center.

These are the cords that will help you more easily find those with whom you need to reconcile imbalances or work through lessons with.

Creative Center: This is one of the seven centers. Its positive pole is resourceful; its negative pole is evocative. It is through this center that ideas, concepts, and thoughts are brought to life. Since it is also the sexual center, it is also the center that aids in the creation of children. (See Centers and Centering)

Cynic: This is one of the seven attitudes. Its positive pole is contradiction; its negative pole is denigration. Cynics view the world in terms of what isn't working, or of what won't work. They will always find flaws in any idea, concept, or plan.

Discarnate: Not incarnate; not in a physical body.

Discrimination: This is one of the seven goals. Its positive pole is sophistication; its negative pole is prejudice. It is used during lifetimes in which you want to emphasize critical faculties. It can help you analyze situations and events, or it can polarize your point of view.

Dominance: This is one of the seven goals. Its positive pole is leadership; its negative pole is dictatorship. It is used for lifetimes that emphasize winning and helping others to win.

Ego: This is the blending of those traits chosen and those traits learned or enculturated.

Emotional Center: This is one of the seven centers. Its positive pole is sensibility; its negative pole is sentimentality. The heart chakra is your emotional energy center. (See Centers and Centering)

Energy: The fundamental substance of everything in the universe. The basis of who and what we are. (See Essence)

Entity: A collection of essences whose purpose (to experience and grow) is similar in intent. Members of an entity support and help each other because their vibrations and energies are similar and sympathetic.

Entity Mate: Entity members are those souls with whom you have participated in physical plane experiences over many lifetimes. They are the same souls who populate your "plays" every time you create a physical life. While they may not always be close to you, being a part of your entity gives them a similar harmonic to yours that creates a comfortable atmosphere not found with other souls.

Essence: The true you. The energy, awareness, and sentience that is you. It is also referred to as the soul. (See Energy)

Essence Contact: This occurs when the personality makes a direct connection with either its own essence or the essence of another person. Essence contact is necessary for spiritual growth to occur. It can be a powerful and life-changing experience, or it can be a relatively mild experience that shifts or broadens your perspective to help you understand your life's goals.

Essence Cycle: *See Soul Cycle*

Essence Level: *See Soul Level*

Essence Twin (also called a Soul Twin or Twin Flame): An essence twin (or twin flame or soul twin) is a soul whose energies are most like yours, due to being identical in all instances except personality and entity.

Essence twins are never from the same entity, but they are always the same essence role and vibrational group...except for scholars. Since scholars are a neutral role (which enables them to shift their frequency and make it harmonious with almost all other essence roles), their essence twin can be any other role, though their preference is kings, warriors, and other scholars. (My essence twin is a late fourth cycle sage-cast warrior with a goal of discrimination in aggression mode and a chief fear of arrogance.)

Since other roles are unable to shift their frequencies, they twin only with those of the same type (warriors with warriors, artisans with artisans, etc.).

The essence twin is a mirror image. It is the closest to true acceptance that one can find in the physical plane. The same innate qualities that make you 'you,' are also what comprise the twin.

Many essence twins will actually come into the physical plane as twins (siblings) so that the love and support can last the entire lifetime. Others will come together later and remain together. Even when essence twins never meet or are not both incarnate, the bond of loving, accepting, and support is still there.

Essence twins, when incarnate or when only one is incarnate, are usually linked at all centers, but are always linked at the thorax, heart, brow, and Tao. This allows them to love, accept, and support one another whether they ever physically meet or not. It is also why when they do meet the rapport is instantaneous.

The term "essence twin" is often mistaken for "soul mate;" however, this is not what is meant by the term. While essence twins can become marital partners, most times the idea of marrying a mirror image of yourself becomes too frightening.

False Personality: This is the part of self that is motivated by fear. It is usually referred to as filters, personality, or ego. It is the part of you that most people think of as their true selves since they don't recognize essence or their soul as a viable being.

Filters: These are the traits chosen by essence for the life being lived. These are the personality traits that overlay the essence. They are usually chosen before a lifetime begins to facilitate the purposes of that lifetime and they only operate for that lifetime. They include the goal, mode, attitude, center, and chief fear. The soul age and essence role are the last two filters, but they are chosen at the beginning of the soul's physical journey and are not discarded until the soul has finished all its lifetimes in the physical world.

Final Cycle Soul: This is the last life to be experienced by a soul. A final cycle soul has chosen to complete its physical plane experiences and, provided the fragment has achieved balance, the soul will no longer return to the physical plane.

Fragment: This is one piece of the overall essence that is you. The essence that is you exists in more realities than just the one you call reality. In each, (reality) there exists a physical representation of you, and inside that physical form is a fragment of your soul. For instance, every time you make a major choice in your life (to marry or not to marry), a fragment of you populates the timeline that you did not select. No choice is ignored. Each one is explored by you, even if is not part of your chosen reality.

Frequency: The rate at which the soul vibrates rated on a scale of one to one hundred. It gives the essence its consistency. Slow frequencies feel more solid, medium frequencies feel more liquid, and fast frequencies feel more gaseous. Each plane of existence and each alternate reality vibrates at a different frequency. That is why we cannot always see or perceive the other realities or planes of existence that are occurring around us.

Goal: This is one of the filters. The goal is a person's primary motivator. The seven goals are re-evaluation, growth, discrimination, acceptance, submission, dominance, and stagnation.

Greed: This is one of the seven chief fears, or obstacles. Its positive pole is egotism; its negative pole is voracity. It is caused by a fear of not having enough of something, such as money, food, sex, or attention.

Growth: This is one of the seven goals. Its positive pole is comprehension; its negative pole is confusion. It is used for lifetimes emphasizing the learning of new things. People with growth as their goal seek stimulation and motivation in order to learn and grow or to experience fear and confusion.

Idealist: This is one of the seven attitudes. Its positive pole is coalescence; its negative pole is abstraction. Idealists view the world in terms of how it could be changed for the better rather than accepting it for how it is. They are never satisfied with the status quo and are always seeking change.

Imbalance: This is sometimes referred to as karma. It is when you add to or remove from someone's wanted choices in a particular life. This creates an imbalance between you which is usually corrected in one or more other lifetimes, or it can be worked through during astral plane intervals.

Impatience: This is one of the seven chief fears, or obstacles. Its positive pole is audacity; its negative pole is intolerance. It is the fear of missing out. Someone with impatience never has enough time to do everything. If spending time with you, they are always convinced they are missing out on something else.

(This is sometimes confused with greed if a person is greedy for time.)

Imprinting: Training, teaching, or conditioning by parents, educators, religious groups, or society in general.

Incarnate: Living in a physical body in the physical world.

Instinctive (or Root) Center: This is one of the seven energy centers. Its positive pole is origin; its negative pole is anatomic (concerned only with the body). (See Centers and Centering)

Intellectual (or Mental) Center: This is one of the seven energy centers. Its positive pole is thought; its negative pole is reason. (See Centers and Centering)

Interactive (or Communications) Center: This is one of the seven energy centers. Its positive pole is reply and the negative is opinion. (See Centers and Centering)

Internal Milestones: These are milestones of awareness. They mark the progress of the fragment as it progresses through the development cycle of the current life. There are seven internal milestones that a fragment passes through in each life. They are:

1. Birth

2. **Me and not me** (recognition of different people, which usually occurs around age 2)

3. **Self-actualization** (the discarding of rules, traditions, and enculturations not wanted, and the accepting of other rules, traditions, and enculturations more acceptable, which occurs between the ages of 16 and 21)

4. **Self-discovery** (the sloughing off of those attributes, trainings, and false personality traits that no longer fit; the taking on of only those filters and traits that fit the goals and lessons of the life. This occurs between the ages of 30 and 50)

5. **Review** (the contemplation of the life as to what was done vs. what was wanted to be accomplished, and then reconciling oneself with the results)

6. **Onset of Death** (this occurs whenever the fragment chooses)

7. **Death** (this also occurs whenever the fragment chooses)

Karma: The abrogating of or the adding to of someone's life choices. This creates an imbalance between you which is usually corrected in one or more other lifetimes, or it can be worked through during astral plane intervals. Karma is a lack of balance, not a punishment.

Intention must exist for an action to become a karmic one; otherwise, it is most likely an accident (and accidents can and do occur on the physical plane).

Karma is an imbalance in energies caused through the addition or abrogation of another's life choices without their permission. If you have an agreement to kill someone, but you make it more painful than was agreed to, you have created an imbalance. If you give someone a million dollars when they planned on a life of hardship and poverty, you owe them, because you have now given them choices they did not plan for. This then, is karma.

To balance the energies entails an understanding of how the original situation went wrong and a replaying of that situation in reverse. That means, the other person now gives you choices that you did not plan for.

Another way to reconcile the imbalance is to understand and acknowledge the original situation; then understand and acknowledge how it created imbalances and agree to let it go. The energies will then move back into balance without the situation being lived again in reverse. This acknowledgement may not be on a conscious level, it may only occur at an essence level; but if both participants fully understand, then the lesson is learned and balance is restored.

Karma is the moving of energies, back and forth, from balance to imbalance and back. It is also the

TA Sullivan

understanding of how and why those energies move
that comprise the full lesson. It is not enough to know
that there is imbalance; you also need to know how
and why the energies move for the lessons of the
physical plane to be completed.

King: This is one of the seven essence roles. The king
seeks to lead and mandate. Other souls will often seek
out kings to be given orders, because the word of the
king carries profound impact. As such, most kings
seek positions of authority, whether it be as
corporation presidents, intensive-care-unit nurses, or
orchestra conductors. The positive pole of the king
essence is mastery, the negative is tyranny.

Lessons (Monads): Lessons are life situations that
you agree to participate in with someone. If you take
the position of student (as in the teacher/student
lesson), then the next time you will be the teacher and
the other person will be the student. Life lessons
usually take the bulk of the lifetime to complete.

Martyrdom: This is one of the seven chief fears, or
obstacles. Its positive pole is selflessness; its negative
pole is mortification. It is the fear of being forgotten or
going unnoticed (when alive or dead). Many
controlling mothers are suffering from martyrdom.

Maya: This is a fear-driven illusion or false belief,
particularly on the soul level (as opposed to false
personality). It is a Hindu term referring to the
transitory, illusory appearance of the physical world

that obscures the spiritual reality from which it originates.

Mental Plane: This is one of the seven planes of existence. This plane's energy is about wisdom and enlightenment. The seventh cycle soul who incarnated as Lao-tzu was linked to and taught from this plane.

Messianic Plane: This is one of the seven planes of existence. The energy of the Messianic plane is focused on agape. Jesus, as a man, was linked to this plane and many of his early teachings were greatly influenced by this link. This is the plane closest to the Tao (or the All).

Milestones: See *Internal Milestones*

Mode: This is one of the seven filters. The mode is a person's primary way of operating. The seven modes are reserve, passion, caution, power, perseverance, aggression, and observation.

Monad: A monad is a framework and model for those souls on the physical plane. Each monad causes the souls participating to experience the physical world from a distinct perspective, yet it allows the participants the freedom to select for themselves how they will handle the experience. Once completed from both sides the participants do not have to do this experience (this monad) again, unless any of them wishes to.

Monads are divided into the types of experiences to be
gained. All lessons not geared toward survival, are
geared toward some type of relationship—
relationships with a person (mother, friend, daughter,
co-worker), relationships with a physical plane
concept (dealing with companies, money, power,
fame, religion, etc.), or relationships with self—
fat/thin (body type disgust or fascination/fixation),
smart/stupid (intelligence fascination), pretty/ugly, etc.

These are your primary monads or lessons, and it is
through these that all physical life can be experienced.
(See Lessons)

Observation: This is one of the seven modes. Its
positive pole is clarity; its negative pole is
surveillance. In observation mode, one releases energy
neutrally.

Oversoul: This is an extensive range of frequencies or
tonalities. While they wish to participate in the
physical plane, they do not wish to do so as fragments
(or souls). Instead, they direct one or more species, the
planet itself, the planet's weather, or other parts of the
set that complete the play taking place in the physical
world.

While dogs, cats, birds, etc., have some awareness,
they are overall directed as a group by several
oversouls (containing well over a million entities in
each oversoul).

Passion: This is one of the seven modes. Its positive pole is self-actualization; its negative pole is identification. In passion mode, one releases energy boundlessly outward.

Perseverance: This is one of the seven modes. Its positive pole is persistence; its negative pole is immutability. In perseverance, one releases energy steadfastly.

Personality: This consists of those traits learned and enculturated through schools, parents, family, churches, and society.

The essence of the soul is the real you. Personality is drama. Personality is a way of looking at and participating in the world. Personality focuses your perceptions and frames your actions and reactions. (See Ego)

Physical Plane: This is one of the densest of the seven planes; it is also where we presently reside. On this plane we learn lessons that can only occur in this realm.

Planes: There are seven planes of existence. They are the Physical, the Astral, the Causal, the Mental, the Buddhic, the Messianic, and the All (or Tao).

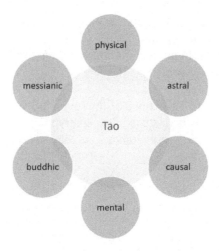

Within each plane is seven levels. Each is a different layer of color, sound, lessons, and growth. Each layer of each plane has a different vibrational rate, all of which comprise the plane's vibrational range. Each layer of the astral plane is within a specific vibrational range, just as each layer of the physical plane is within a specific vibrational frequency. This links all the layers of a plane together, while keeping each of the planes separated from each.

On the astral plane, the lessons are focused on reviewing the physical plane experiences but from an emotional point of view. This is because the astral plane is primarily about experiencing emotions. On the causal plane they study truths—personal, global, universal, and pandimensional truths.

On the Mental plane they study thoughts in all their various forms. They use thoughts and the energy behind the thoughts to create their versions of realities, art, trouble, and beauty.

In the Messianic plane they study perception, dreams, and realities—the creating of, connecting of, and manipulating of. It is on this plane that they experiment with reality and perception, and with putting thought and emotion together to get something beyond words.

The Buddhic plane uses lights, sound (music, tone) to create the different realities of that plane, and then experiment and experience those realities. They combine these experiences and creations with their experiences and creations learned on the previous planes.

Poles: Two aspects of an energy center. The positive pole is an energy center's true or love-based manifestation. The negative pole is the distortion or constriction of that energy by fear. It is always the middle point, the balanced point, that we should seek.

Power: This is one of the seven modes. Its positive pole is authority; its negative pole is oppression. In power mode, one releases energy strongly.

Pragmatist: This is one of the seven attitudes. Its positive pole is practicality; its negative pole is dogma. Pragmatists see the world in terms of what works best or most efficiently.

Priest: This is one of the seven essence roles chosen by newly formed souls. The priest seeks to serve the higher good, whatever the priest conceives the higher good to be. The priest desires to succor, counsel, and uplift; the priest also seeks to preach, and will seek work that will permit such service, or work that can be used to that end. The positive pole of the priest is compassion; the negative is zeal.

Realist: This is one of the seven attitudes. Its positive pole is perception; its negative pole is supposition. Realists view the world in terms of what is; they attempt to focus on a situation's objective facts.

Re-Evaluation: This is one of the seven goals. Its positive pole is atavism or simplicity; its negative pole is withdrawal. It is used for lifetimes spent processing past experiences.

Reincarnation: The idea that our soul lives multiple lifetimes, gaining experience and insight during each of these lives.

Reserved: This is one of the seven modes. Its positive pole is restraint; its negative pole is inhibition. In reserve mode, one draws energy inward and upward, in a contained manner.

Roles (in essence): There are seven essence roles that a newly formed soul can choose from. They are server, artisan, warrior, scholar, sage, priest, and king.

Each soul selects one of these seven essence roles and retains that role for each of its physical incarnations. This role becomes part of the being's vibrational range that affects the way in which the soul experiences the physical world.

Sage: This is one of the seven essence roles chosen when the soul is first created. The sage seeks communication in all things. Therefore, they are drawn to all forms of entertainment, including politics and the law, as well as religion. The positive pole of the sage is expression; the negative is oration (oration is considered negative because it is usually someone speaking just to hear their own voice).

Scholar: This is one of the seven essence roles chosen when the soul is first created. This is a neutral role, and as such, is more capable of understanding all the other roles more fully. The scholar essence seeks knowledge and tends to regard life as an experiment. They are drawn to informational occupations, and to the contemplative life. The positive pole of the scholar is knowledge, the negative is theory. (Theories are only a way to avoid making decisions or facing reality unless you come up with a way to invoke the theory.)

Self-deprecation: This is one of the seven chief fears, or obstacles. Its positive pole is humility; its negative pole is abasement. It is a fear of being inadequate. Someone with self-deprecation will always see themselves as inadequate, and every time they fail to complete a task (no matter the reason) their viewpoint is then reinforced for them.

Self-destruction: This is one of the seven chief fears, or obstacles. Its positive pole is self-sacrifice; its negative pole is immolation. It is the fear of being unworthy. Someone with a chief fear of self-destruction is always going to see the world as better off without them. This may lead them to make great sacrifices to save those deemed more worthy, or it may cause the person to simply give up.

Server: This is one of the seven essence roles chosen when the soul is created.

The server essence seeks to serve the common good, whatever the server determines that to be. As such, these souls are often drawn to the educational, medical, diplomatic, bureaucratic, and serving professions. The positive pole of the server essence is service, the negative is bondage.

Skeptic: This is one of the seven attitudes. Its positive pole is investigation; its negative pole is suspicion. Skeptics always view the world with doubt.

Soul: This is one piece of the overall essence that is you. You exist in more realities than just this one, and within each you in those other realities, there exists a fragment of your soul. Reincarnation merely represents the probabilities in a time context; that is, portions of yourselves that are materialized in (to you) an historical context.

Soul Cycle: Soul Cycles and Soul Levels (these pertain only to the essence, not the physical body). There are seven physical plane cycles with seven levels each; however, only five cycles incarnate regularly. Sixth and seventh cycles rarely incarnate, and only when momentous changes are needed within the physical plane. (Each level is equivalent to many lifetimes. It may take 10, 20, or more lifetimes to complete a single level for a single cycle.)

The cycle and level are based on the last lessons completed successfully. (This only means that no imbalances were created during the lesson or that all the participants are happy with the outcome of the lessons.)

> **First Cycles** are terrified of almost everything. If they perceive the world as hostile, they will either respond with violence or by completely withdrawing. They truly do not know the "rules" of life, but they can learn. They are very attuned to the other planes of existence and to the All.

> **Second Cycles** lack understanding and depth, but are very aware of society's and life's rules, and will try not to vary from them. Viewpoints that differ from theirs and what they perceive as right, will cause them to respond with confusion and belligerence. They have begun to lose some of their "other worldly" connections as they turn their focus to the world in which they now reside.

> **Third Cycles** are the most attuned to the physical world and the life it offers. They perceive the

world as a challenge and the objects such as money, fame, or possessions, as the ultimate prizes to be won. They have little or no appreciation for or connection with any world beyond the one in which they live. Death is to be avoided because it interferes with the pursuit of their physical life.

Fourth Cycles are more concerned with family and community. Their focus is turned more inward, away from the physical world and they begin to see the competitiveness as less important. They have begun to reconnect with the other worlds and with the All. They feel a longing but are unsure as to what it is they seek.

Fifth Cycles are concerned with being and the search for truth. (Truth is different for everyone, but they usually search for the universal truths, not the personal truths.) They usually seek the path of least resistance and realize that most problems are only those caused by personality. Most late-level fifth cycles can see the games and so avoid the dramas. They are reconnecting with those no longer incarnate.

Sixth Cycles are rare visitors to the physical world. Their presence usually causes great social upheavals.

Seventh Cycles create global upheavals. Their presence in the physical world creates changes on a global scale. The last recognized seventh cycle to Earth was the soul that stepped into Jesus' body, and for 30 days shared his esoteric views with the world.

Soul Cycle Levels: Each growth cycle has seven levels:

1st Levels respond at essence without any real perception of the nature of their actions.

2nd Levels begin to learn response and comparison.

3rd Levels begin to consider the consequences of their actions. They learn discernment and evaluation.

4th Levels begin to gather all their knowledge together and build themselves a foundation.

5th Levels start to integrate all their experiences and learning from previous levels.

6th Levels become aware of the many obligations that they have—whether it be karmic or other types of lessons and agreements.

7th Levels remember and reflect on all that was learned and begin to teach others.

Soul Flow or Soul Creation: A core of soul energy flows from the Tao to the Messianic plane. Here they work on various tasks. A Congregation of soul energy may decide to move into the Buddhic plane to work on things there. From there a Collection of soul energy may move on to the Mental plane. If lessons are wanted to be learned on the causal plane, then a Cadre may form and move to that location.

Entities (smaller groups of soul energy) can move on to the astral plane. These entities create sparks (or souls) that then either stay together on the astral plane as crews, split up—some staying on the astral and others creating lives and experiences on the physical plane, or they can all experience life on the physical plane.

Soul Twin (Essence Twin or Twin Flames): A soul twin (or twin flame or essence twin) is a soul whose energies are most like yours, due to being identical in all instances except personality and entity.

Essence twins are never from the same entity, but they are always the same essence role and vibrational group...except for scholars. Since scholars are a neutral role (which enables them to shift their frequency and make it harmonious with almost all other essence roles), their essence twin can be any other role, though their preference is kings, warriors, and other scholars. (My essence twin is a late fourth cycle sage-cast warrior with a goal of discrimination in aggression mode and a chief fear of arrogance.)

Since other roles are unable to shift their frequencies, they twin only with those of the same type (warriors with warriors, artisans with artisans, etc.).

The essence twin is a mirror image. It is the closest to true acceptance that one can find in the physical plane.

The same innate qualities that make you 'you,' are also what comprise the twin.

Many essence twins will actually come into the physical plane as twins (siblings) so that the love and support can last the entire lifetime. Others will come together later and remain together. Even when essence twins never meet or are not both incarnate, the bond of loving, accepting, and support is still there.

Essence twins, when incarnate or when only one is incarnate, are usually linked at all centers, but are always linked at the thorax, heart, brow, and Tao. This allows them to love, accept, and support one another whether they ever physically meet or not. It is also why when they do meet the rapport is instantaneous.

The term "essence twin" is often mistaken for "soul mate;" however, this is not what is meant by the term. While essence twins can become marital partners, most times the idea of marrying a mirror image of yourself becomes too frightening.

Spiritual Center: This is one of the seven centers. The positive pole is unification and the negative pole is intuition. It is also referred to as the crown or the Tao chakra. (See Centering)

Spiritualist: This is one of the seven attitudes. Its positive pole is verification; its negative pole is faith. Spiritualists view the world in terms of its possibilities.

Stagnation: This is one of the seven goals. Its positive pole is suspension or free flowing; its negative pole is inertia (the unwillingness to take any action). It is used for lifetimes of rest or of learning to let go.

Stoic: This is one of the seven attitudes. Its positive pole is tranquility (this is the acceptance of life and everything it entails). The negative pole is resignation (resignation means you give up on everything). Stoics view the world with serenity, feeling that outer events aren't of primary importance.

Stubbornness: This is one of the seven chief fears, or obstacles. Its positive pole is determination; its negative pole is obstinacy. It is a fear of change.

Submission: This is one of the seven goals. Its positive pole is devotion; its negative pole is subservience. It is used for lifetimes that emphasize supporting a greater cause.

Tao: Also known as All That Is. This is the awareness of being, the overall consciousness of sentience. It is the sentient energy from which all things were created—people, animals, the planet, light, heat, chairs, windows, everything.

Warrior: This is one of the seven essence roles. The warrior essence seeks a challenge. By nature, the warrior essence is intensely loyal, both as friend and foe. Warriors are drawn to professions that encourage activity and provide challenges including armed services especially during the third and fourth cycles.

The positive pole of the warrior essence is persuasion, the negative is coercion.

Available at all online book outlets:

CHOICES
Insights on Life and Relationships

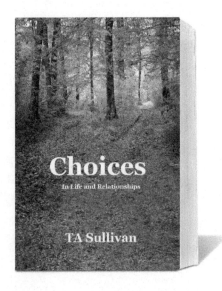

Another award-winning book by TA Sullivan.

This book, which works well as a companion to *Escorting the Dead*, provides more insights and wisdom from the masters.

The masters explain how life is an intricate pattern of relationships, which we weave into and out of our lives with every choice we make. They speak about how our choices are based in love or fear (love's opposite), and how we can help ourselves overcome the fear to make more love-based choices.

They also discuss the distinct types and levels of relationships that we create during our lifetimes, and how each of these relationships affect the experiences we have.

It is a compilation of questions, answers, and explanations that (hopefully) will help you gain a new perspective to and understanding for the complexities of human relationships.

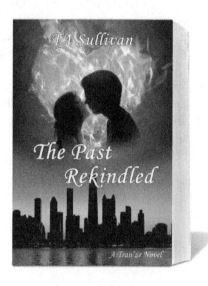

people move on–even if it means bending those rules a bit.

In the real world, I'm stuck working with my high school crush. Although he hurt and betrayed me back then, I've always wondered what would have happened if we had gotten together. Is it too late, or should I take the risk?

To find out the answers, buy the book *The Past Rekindled* by TA Sullivan. Available at all online booksellers.

About the Author

THIS AWARD-WINNING author was born in the back of a cab, and since then she has continued to be unconventional in all that she does.

When she's not busy writing, she's exploring the astral realms or studying quantum theories.

Because of her avid interest in philosophy, metaphysics, and the paranormal, she began compiling dream symbols and their meanings when she was a teenager. She has released that compilation into the comprehensive and award-winning book, *On Dreams and Dream Symbols*. It is one of the largest dream dictionaries of its kind.

She has also used her interest in writing and the paranormal to create a fantasy series, *Darkwind of Danaria*. The first two books, *The Starstone* and *The Globe of Souls*, are available now at all online book outlets.

Her award-winning book detailing her near death experience, *Escorting the Dead*, and the companion book, *Choices,* have led to numerous speaking engagements. She also answers questions on the Q&A forum, *Quora*, and she offers Life Readings (which include information regarding past, current, and future lives) at https://tasreadings.wordpress.com.

Write a Review

ALL AUTHORS NEED reviews. It lets us know that you read and enjoyed our books. So, help me out by going to any of the more popular book sites and writing review on my books.

Follow her at:
>Twitter (@tasinator)
>Facebook
>LinkedIn

Visit her website at:
>https://taslookingglass.wordpress.com/
>or
>https://tasreadings.wordpress.com/

Made in the USA
Monee, IL
24 August 2021

76419466R00187